THIS TIMELY book presents a comprehensive analysis of the most disturbing constitutional and ethical questions facing
Americans today—majority rule and minority rights. Judge Asch provides a
thoughtful and probing, yet balanced picture of how both rights and responsibilities under the Constitution affect such
pressing, controversial issues as race
relations, ownership of firearms, censorship of the press, recent obscenity rulings, picketing and other activities of
organized labor, restriction of protest
demonstrations, public financial support
of private religious schools, prayer in
public schools, rights of conscientious
objectors, treatment of alcoholics and
narcotics addicts, and virtually the entire
litany of our present-day problems.

SIDNEY H. ASCH is a Judge of the Civil
Court of the City of New York and a member
of the graduate faculties of the City University of New York and Mount Sinai Medical
School where, among other subjects, he lectures on Psychiatry and the Law. He holds a
Ph.D. degree in sociology and was a member
of the New York State Legislature for ten
years as well as on the faculty of the New
York Law School.

CIVIL RIGHTS AND RESPONSIBILITIES UNDER THE CONSTITUTION

KNOW YOUR LAW

Civil Rights
& Responsibilities
under the
Constitution

SIDNEY H. ASCH

New York

Published by ARCO PUBLISHING COMPANY, Inc.
219 Park Avenue South, New York, N. Y. 10003
Copyright © Sidney H. Asch, 1968

Library of Congress Catalog Card Number 68-19522

Arco Book Number 668-01761-9

Printed in the United States of America

Foreword

Not too long ago, Justice William Brennan, Jr., of the United States Supreme Court, in speaking to a group of school administrators, urged them to involve themselves more seriously in making sure that the Bill of Rights is being taught properly. He deplored the fact that many young people know little or nothing about the first ten amendments and that many students who did know, no longer have confidence in these guarantees.

It is easy to concur with Justice Brennan's evaluation of the situation, and at the same time, to offer one addendum. Ignorance of the history and nature of our constitutional rights and responsibilities, lack of conviction in its potency, are not limited to the young. The first ten amendments to the Constitution of the United States, like the Ten Commandments, are blithely assumed to be the cherished possession of every American. Yet, this is far from the case.

Judge Asch has sought to meet the need for information concerning the nature and background of our constitutional rights and responsibilities. He has written a simple, yet accurate, exposition of the provisions of the Constitution relating to this field, as well as the significance of some of the leading cases. In addition, he explains how the Supreme Court has evolved so as to shape both the substance and procedure in the field of constitutional law so as to meet the demands of a changing American society.

He explains the genesis of many civil rights concepts and how they have met some of the most disturbing ethical and legal issues of our day. In language understandable to laymen, he discusses such constitutional issues as school prayers, censorship of the press and recent obscenity rulings, protest demonstrations,

5

conscientious objectors and their methods, the use of firearms, picketing, and a whole range of additional subjects that touch upon civil rights and responsibilities. He clarifies how the constitutional framework has accommodated itself during the two centuries that have elapsed since the founding fathers framed the Constitution. Judge Asch evaluates the impact of the "Warren Court" and raises important questions about the future direction of the work of the Supreme Court. What is most impressive is the way in which Judge Asch has managed to provide the comprehensive and informative coverage of rights and responsibilities in his book.

It is significant that Sidney Asch has underscored civil responsibilities, as well as rights. Many people, old as well as young, seem very solicitious about their own rights and the responsibilities of others, but they look no further. Our American system rests on a mutuality of rights and duties.

The Bill of Rights opens by granting freedom of religion, of speech, of the press, of assembly, of petition. Yet, as Chief Justice Warren pointed out in an address delivered as part of the James Madison series at the New York University School of Law: "Members of a free society are called upon to bear an extraordinarily heavy responsibility, for such a society is based upon the *reciprocal self-imposed discipline* of *both the governed and their government.*"

The Chief Justice went on: "Many nations in the past have attempted to develop democratic institutions, only to lose them when either the people or their government lapsed from the *vigorous self-control* that is essential to the maintenance of a proper relation between freedom and order. Such failure has produced the totalitarianism or the anarchy that, however masked, are the mortal enemies of an ordered society."

Civil Rights and Responsibilities Under the Constitution is a step in the direction of recognizing the duality of freedom and law in a democracy.

ROBERT M. MORGENTHAU

Contents

CIVIL RIGHTS AND RESPONSIBILITIES UNDER THE CONSTITUTION

1. The Historic Sources

ALMOST TWO HUNDRED years ago, in words which still live today as they did for the hardy souls who dared to invade this continent and to create this nation, the Declaration of Independence expressed confidence in a political system which would give recognition and protection to the rights of ordinary men and women against encroachment by arbitrary government. Because of the very real deprivations and sufferings which our Founding Fathers had endured in the lands from which they fled to find refuge in the New World, they clung to their belief in these "inalienable rights," refusing to regard them as merely some abstract ideal of government or justice.

EUROPEAN ORIGINS

It is a cliché to say that we take our freedoms for granted; yet, like many clichés, this one expresses a good deal of truth. Although we know that our forbears suffered and died for their freedom, few people are quite sure of exactly how our liberties were gained. We blithely and uncritically assume that these freedoms cannot be taken from us because they were secured by dedicated spirits who overcame a tyrannical govern-

13

ment nearly two centuries ago. However, the history of the twentieth century belies this belief that individual rights, individual liberties, are sacred and cannot be wrested from our grasps. If we are to preserve our civil rights and liberties, we must develop an understanding of their origins.

Recognition of the sacredness of each individual man, woman, and child did not come quickly. Primitive peoples generally regarded a person as part of the tribal community, not as an individual—a person separate from the group. The great prophets and philosophers of the Orient conceived of man as being part of a broad river of humanity, which flowed into an enormous ocean of life extending into eternity. The individual counted as little in such a scheme of things. It was only with the Greek and Jewish traditions and, later, with the Christian ideals that the human being began to be regarded as a single person, significant in his own right. Each person was believed to have been endowed with a gift of freedom by a Divinity, a God who concerned Himself with promoting the fullest development of each of His creatures. As the beliefs of the Jews, the Greeks, and the Christians were spread throughout the world, the ideal of the sanctity of individual rights began to take root. These concepts were not accepted with equanimity. They were secured at the cost of suffering, of struggling, of the lives of people who sacrificed themselves to establish the rights and freedoms which they believed were their due. However, in countries influenced by the Jewish and Christian philosophies, certain ideas gradually came to be respected. These ideas involved the following basic concepts:

- the right to free expression and, as a corollary, the right to stand mute and not be compelled to testify or to speak against oneself

- the right to freedom of religion, which ultimately came to mean that government would not support any single church

- the right to seek changes in the established society or government and, for that purpose, to assemble to assert one's grievances
- the right to the protection of life and property against arbitrary seizure by government officials
- the right to a trial by a jury consisting of people of the same sort as the person to be tried
- the right to be secure against physical torture such as blinding, mutilation, burning—in short, against all cruel and unusual punishment
- the right to have a lawyer when facing indictments brought by government officials

These revolutionary ideas precipitated a revolt against the rulers of England, France, and Germany. The cries for individual freedom resulted in bloody wars, the dethroning and killing of kings, and the ignominious and painful deaths of thousands.

COLONIAL ORIGINS

In England the Puritans left the Church of England because they were convinced that it had become corrupt. Some of these Puritans, as well as other persons who could not accept the political and religious practices of the day, fled to Holland and, later, from there to North America where they established colonies on the shores of the Massachusetts Bay.

These settlers felt that their essential rights as Englishmen, painfully won in earlier generations, were being stolen from them in England by kings who disregarded Parliament and refused to call it into session. Between 1620 and 1640, under aegis of the Puritan movement, more than twenty-five thousand men and women migrated to what eventually came to be called New England. Later, after Parliament had been reconvened in England in 1640, some of these Puritans returned to their homeland. But the many who remained in Massachusetts and elsewhere could never forget their vision of independence, and it was this that laid the ideological foundation for the American Revolution.

During this time of immigrant settlement in America a group of Catholics seeking an atmosphere of liberty organized a community in Maryland. There, under a charter given to Lord Calvert, the colony's founder, a representative assembly was set up. This legislative body, similar to the House of Burgesses in the nearby colony of Virginia, claimed the right to enact laws for all free men within its territory.

In neighboring Virginia the colonists asserted the rights and privileges of freeborn Englishmen, including free expression and the right to a trial by jury. The legislative body, the House of Burgesses, asserted, in 1624, that it had the authority to determine the taxation to be imposed in Virginia.

While the Puritans in New England were themselves rigid and intolerant, their struggles planted the seed for the germination in America of the concept of freedom for the individual. The settlers in Maryland, Virginia, Rhode Island, and the other colonies evinced to their royal governors their belief that they were entitled to the same rights afforded to each freeholder under the common law in England. In England the sovereign was believed to have an obligation to protect the free man's life, his liberty, and his property from encroachment. This claim of right went back to the twelfth century when the right to jury trial, to the assistance of a lawyer, to be released on bail, and to be protected from excessive fines found legal validation.

The one hundred fifty years which succeeded the establishment of settlements in Massachusetts, Virginia, Maryland, and other places in America were ones of constant struggle by the colonists—not only against the vicissitudes of nature and the threat of the Indians, but also against the kings of England and the royal governors who wanted to keep the settlers under absolute domination. The early democracy of Virginia was overthrown by the incoming Royalist group, and the power of government gradually went over into the hands of the royal governor and his Council. In the colonies of New England the ground swell of enthusiasm for democratic government created constant conflict with the powers of the royal governors.

Late in the seventeenth century when James II became the king of England, he merged all of the New England colonies into one province. Sir Edmund Andros was appointed as governor general of the entire province. Andros was given virtually all the authority of a totalitarian dictator, and King James excised from the new charter all of the provisions which might have provided for popular representation.

However, in 1688, after England's famous Glorious Revolution—the revolt of Parliament against the King which brought an end to absolute monarchy in England—the colonists boldly took steps to regain their popular form of government. Patriots in Boston and nearby communities seized Governor Andros and held him prisoner. They captured the English fort in the harbor of Boston. As a result of these developments a revised charter was granted to Massachusetts in 1691.

Thus, the revolution in England in 1688 was the forerunner of the American Revolution, which was to take place one hundred years later. Certainly, a major factor in the loss of the English throne by King James was his refusal to recognize the rights that Englishmen felt were part of their heritage. In 1689 Parliament adopted a fundamental Declaration of Rights and Liberties which made it illegal for the Crown to suspend laws or to levy taxes without the approval of Parliament.

Foreshadowing the fundamental concepts that were to be expressed by the American Bill of Rights, the Declaration of 1689 enunciated the idea that British subjects had an undeniable right to petition the king without restriction; that freedom of expression and the right to debate in Parliament could not be questioned; that the establishment or maintenance of a standing army in time of peace without the approval of Parliament was illegal. The Declaration further set forth the principle that election of members to Parliament should be held freely and that Parliament itself should be frequently convened for business. This Declaration also made it clear that excessive bail could not be required of any person accused of criminal conduct. In addition, excessive fines could not be required, and cruel and unusual punishments were forbidden. A subject charged with a crime was to be afforded a trial by "impartial jurors," and accused persons could not be subject to fine or forfeiture before conviction. Thus, like the Magna Carta, the Declaration of 1689 was a major step toward clarification of the rights and liberties of all freeborn Englishmen.

The Magna Carta, which had been grudgingly accepted and signed by King John in 1215 at Runnymede, had guaranteed the rights of the feudal barons and other nobles. The great Declaration of 1689 extended this warranty of freedom to a great many more Englishmen.

After James II had been deposed from the throne, William and Mary were required to acknowledge the existence and the validity of the Declaration before they could assume the Crown.

Naturally, the colonists in New England, Maryland, Virginia, and other areas of the New World were convinced that the Declaration of 1689 guaranteed to them, just as to the residents of England, certain basic rights. Their position was sustained by Chief Justice Holt of the highest court in England when, in 1694, he ruled that the rights of Englishmen extended to those in the Colonies. Just twenty-six years later, in 1720, the English attorney general expressed the opinion that the common law of England extended to the Colonies as law unless there was "some private Act to the contrary."

When King George II came to the throne of England, he did not realize that the colonists in America took their rights and privileges as Englishmen very seriously. In 1760 he tried to compel the American colonists to pay higher taxes in spite of the fact that they were not represented in Parliament. The slogan "No taxation without representation" became a rallying cry;

and, as we know now, by 1775 the American colonists were up in arms and in rebellion against Mother England.

Finally, in 1776 the leaders of the American Colonies took the bold step of declaring their independence from England. Speaking for the people of the "United States of America," these leaders called out to the nations to help them against the tyranny of the British Crown. In striking terms they explained their grievances against the oppressive king. They contended that George III and his advisors were guilty of un-British activities, and they argued that George and his ministers had failed to give them the rights to which they were entitled as free Englishmen in the Colonies under the Declaration of 1689.

In their great Declaration of Independence the colonists uttered those magnificent sentiments which have continued to reverberate down through the ages:

> When in the course of human events, it becomes necessary for one people to dissolve the political bands, which have connected them with another, and to assume among the powers of the earth, the separate and equal station to which the laws of nature and of nature's God entitle them, a decent respect to the opinions of mankind requires that they should declare the causes which impel them to the separation. We hold these truths to be self-evident, that all men are created equal, that they are endowed by their creator with certain unalienable rights, that among these are life, liberty and the pursuit of happiness.

THE CONSTITUTION, AS DRAFTED

The Thirteen Colonies joined together in a loose organization under the Articles of Confederation. It had been approved by them between 1778 and 1781 while the army of George Washington was in the field, carrying on its war against the British. Washington earned a great victory for the Americans and for posterity. Yet, it is highly doubtful that the ragtail forces of General Washington would have succeeded without the substantial assistance furnished by France and other friendly allies. There were no funds with which to pay the soldiers of Washington's army on any regular basis. The United States currency rapidly declined in value in spite of efforts to control this depreciation. The Continental Congress did not have the authority to raise taxes, and without tax revenues, financial needs could not be met. States raised tax and trade barriers among themselves. They ignored many of the resolutions adopted by Congress. Foreign nations were in a dilemma as to whether to regard the new United States as a single country or as thirteen individual sovereignties.

A group of businessmen got together in Annapolis in the year 1786 because of concern over conditions. They suggested that Congress convene an assembly of representative citizens to revise or amend the Articles of Confederation. These citizens were quite concerned by what had almost amounted to an insurrection led by Captain Daniel Shays, by the rapid inflation of the United States currency, and by the dangerous signs of a total breakdown in government.

In 1787, on the recommendation of Congress, a convention met to determine what could be done. The delegates were not empowered to draft a new constitution. However, under the encouragement of such leaders as Washington, Franklin, Madison, Mason, Ellsworth, and other persons of property and standing in the colonies they decided to go ahead. Thomas Jefferson and John Adams were abroad on special assignments and could not participate personally in the convention. Nevertheless, they concurred in the idea that it was necessary to set up a stronger central government. Some of America's outstanding men of affairs gathered at Annapolis. This group was perhaps the most capable aggregation of philosopher-activists ever joined together for a single undertaking in the Western world. The Constitution of 1789 was their brainchild, and it is essentially this same Constitution that still acts as a guide for the American federal system today. This master document commences with a preamble which breathes the very spirit of popular rights:

> We, the People of the United States, in order to . . . secure the blessings of liberty to ourselves and our posterity, do ordain and establish this Constitution for the United States of America.

In addition there were many specific articles in the original Constitution which protected civil rights and liberties. For example, the body of the Constitution provided:

> The privilege of habeas corpus shall not be suspended, unless when in cases of rebellion or invasion, the public safety may require it.

> No bill of attainder or *ex post facto* law shall be passed.

> No title of nobility shall be granted by the United States.

> No state . . . shall pass any bill of attainder or *ex post fatco* law, or law impairing the obligation of contract; or grant any title of nobility.

> The trial of all crimes, except in cases of impeachment, shall be by jury; and such trial shall be held in the state where the said crimes shall have been committed.

> Treason against the United States shall consist only in levying war against them, or, in adhering to their enemies, giving them aid and comfort. No person shall be convicted of treason unless on the testimony of two witnesses of the same overt act, or on confession in open court.

> The Congress shall have the power to declare a corruption of blood or forfeiture, except during the life of the person attainted.

> Judgment in cases of impeachment shall not extend further than to remove from office, and to disqualification to hold and enjoy any office of honor, trust or profit under the United States . . .

> The citizens of each state shall be entitled to all the privileges and immunities of citizens in the several states.

> The United States shall guarantee to every state in this union a republican form of government, and shall protect each of

them against invasion; and on application of the legislature, or of the executive (when the legislature cannot be convened), against domestic violence.

No religious tests shall ever be required as a qualification to any office or public trust under the United States.

THE FIRST TEN AMENDMENTS

In spite of these safeguards the advocates of ratification of the Constitution were deluged by criticism when the draft was finally sent to the thirteen original states for approval. In certain key states it was passed by only the slimmest majority. It has been argued by historical experts that, if the people themselves had been permitted to vote on the Constitution, it would have been defeated. Approval was given by the state legislatures only after extensive debates and contention. Those who inveighed against the Constitution made essentially two arguments. First, they contended that the proposed Constitution weakened the power of the states to a great extent, and, second, they felt that it should have an express Bill of Rights.

Thomas Jefferson, the author of the Declaration of Independence, was one of those who felt that the basic Constitution should be strengthened as soon as possible by a charter of personal rights and liberties.

A number of states had already developed their own bills of rights. Probably the most outstanding was the Virginia Declaration of Rights which was largely the work of George Mason, a delegate to the Constitutional Convention. In its initial section this Declaration asserted that property rights were among the foremost of the "inherent rights" with which all men were endowed "by nature." It went on to say:

> All men are, by nature, equally free and independent and have certain inherent rights of which, when they enter into a state of society, they cannot, by any compact, deprive or divest

their posterity; namely, the enjoyment of life and liberty, the means of acquiring and possessing property, and pursuing and obtaining happiness and safety.

Thomas Jefferson, writing from Paris, advised: "A Bill of Rights is what the people are entitled to against every government on earth, general or particular; and what no just government should refuse or rest on inference." He sought provisions "providing clearly, and without the aid of sophism, for freedom of religion, freedom of the press, protection against standing armies, restriction of monopolies, the eternal and unremitting force of the habeas corpus laws, and trials by jury in all manner of fact triable by the law of the land, and not by the laws of nations."

The position of those who defended the Constitution as it was originally drafted was most ardently asserted by Alexander Hamilton. He saw no need for the inclusion of a Bill of Rights in the Constitution. In *The Federalist*, No. 84, he gave his reasons for feeling that the Constitution was effective as it was. Hamilton argued that:

Bills of rights are, in their origin, stipulations between kings and their subjects. Such was the Magna Carta, obtained by the barons, swords in hand, from King John. Such was the subsequent confirmations of that Charter by succeeding princes. Such was the Petition of Right as consented to by Charles I in the beginning of his reign. Such, also, was the Declaration of Right presented by the lords and Commons to the Prince of Orange in 1688, and afterwards thrown into the form of an Act of Parliament, called the Bill of Rights.

It is evident, therefore, that according to the primitive signification, they had no application of Constitutions professedly founded upon the power of the people, and executed by their immediate representatives and servants. Here, in strictness, the people surrender nothing; and as they retain everything they have no need of particular reservations.

These contentions of Alexander Hamilton were certainly worthy of serious consideration. However, the unanswered questions raised by Thomas Jefferson carried the day. As he wrote in one of his articles:

> Is the spirit of the people infallible, a permanent reliance? Is it government? Is this the kind of protection we receive in return for the rights we give up? Besides, the spirit of the times may alter, will alter. Our rulers will become corrupt, our people careless. A single zealot may commence persecution, and better men be his victims. It can never be too often repeated that the time for fixing every essential right on a legal basis is while our rulers are honest and ourselves united.

The first ten amendments were added to the Constitution as a sop to popular concerns; yet, they were also a reflection of the deep-seated convictions of many of the leaders of the infant nation. The provisions of the Bill of Rights protected the individual from government interference with freedom of thought, religion, press, speech, petition, assembly. They also guarded the property and physical security of the individual from abuse by agents of the federal government; and these amendments were very specific, dealing with such things as the right to jury trial, the privilege against self-incrimination, excessive bail and fines, cruel and inhuman punishment, general warrants, unreasonable search and seizure, right to counsel, and compensation for property taken for public use. These are set out in the first eight amendments.

The Ninth and Tenth Amendments are different in nature. The Ninth Amendment is brief and to the point:

> The enumeration in the Constitution of certain rights shall not be construed to deny or disparage others retained by the people.

The Tenth Amendment is also terse and explicit:

> The powers not delegated to the United States by the Constitution, not prohibited by it to the States, are reserved to the States respectively, or to the people.

The Ninth Amendment is simply a reflection of the view of James Madison, as expressed in *The Federalist*, No. 51. "If we advert to the nature of republican government, we shall find that the censorial power is in the people over the government, and not in the government over the people." The Tenth Amendment, which notes the power left to the States, was added to the Constitution to placate those who believed in states rights. Although the Ninth and Tenth Amendments were not specific in marking the line between state and national power, throughout a major part of the history of these United States, most of the vital areas of governmental concern have been left to the states. In the last forty years, however, there has been a marked shift in the allocation and exercise of governmental power. More and more, the national government is extending its interests and operations into problem areas that at one time were the concern of the separate localities. Powers once reserved to the states and to the people are being pre-empted by Washington. Aside from oratory in the legislative halls and in Fourth of July rallies, this trend continues.

AFTER THE CIVIL WAR

As a result of the War Between the States, which came to an end in 1865, three amendments were added to the Constitution, and these increased the rights of Americans immeasurably. These three Civil War amendments were the Thirteenth Amendment, which abolished slavery; the Fourteenth Amendment, which made all persons born in the United States citizens of the United States and of the state in which they lived; and the Fifteenth Amendment, which provided that the vote should not be taken from any citizen because of "race, color, or previous condition of servitude."

Each one of these amendments included a clause which authorized Congress to enforce the amendment "by appropriate legislation." So far, Congress has exercised this mandate only to a limited degree.

In 1919 the right to vote was extended to women by means of the Nineteenth Amendment. In 1964 the right of suffrage was further guaranteed by the Twenty-Fourth Amendment, which abolished the poll tax and similar restrictive measures.

Even superficial examination of the body of the Constitution, the Bill of Rights, and the amendments gives assurance that a major premise of the American constitutional system is an overwhelming concern for freedom. Study of the historic sources of the American Constitution makes this clear.

2. Civil Rights in the Supreme Court

EVERY OBSERVER of the American political scene is struck by the puissance of the United States Supreme Court. In 1848, Alexis de Tocqueville wrote, "Scarcely any political question arises in the United States that is not resolved sooner or later into a judicial question." About one hundred years later, Harold J. Laski commented, "The respect in which the federal courts and, above all, the Supreme Court are held is hardly surpassed by the influence they exert on the life of the United States." How is it that the justices occupy such a strategic position? Undoubtedly, in substantial measure it derives from the power of the Supreme Court to interpret and apply the Constitution.

THE JURISDICTION OF THE SUPREME COURT

The justices of the Supreme Court are not simply black-robed oracles, available to answer the conundrums submitted to them. They are authorized only to decide actual cases between adverse parties, rather than to respond to general inquiries concerning a word or phrase of the Constitution or the meaning of a statute.

There are very few legal matters which can be initiated in

27

the Supreme Court. For the most part, the jurisdiction of the Court is to hear appeals from lower courts. Congress has empowered the Court to review certain decisions of both state and federal courts. If, in the settlement of a law suit, the highest court in a state has declared a federal law or treaty unconstitutional or has upheld a state law against the contention that it violates the U.S. Constitution or a federal law or treaty, the Supreme Court *must* review the case on appeal if the losing party so wishes. In all other state cases involving federal questions, the party seeking review can only petition for a writ of certiorari, which the Supreme Court may or may not grant. The rule is similar with respect to federal cases. Only when a federal court of appeals invalidates a state law because it is contrary to a federal law or treaty or to the Constitution, must the decision be reviewed by the Supreme Court. In all other cases the losing party may petition the Supreme Court to issue a writ of certiorari. Most petitions for a writ are denied because they do not present questions to which the Court wishes to address itself or because of the pressure of other Court business.

Perhaps even more significant than the assertion by the Court of the power to review acts of Congress, is the authority which the United States Supreme Court and other federal courts have exercised over state laws and decisions by state courts. The Court has invalidated less than a hundred statutes of Congress; however, it has struck down hundreds of state acts.

THE DOCTRINE OF JUDICIAL REVIEW

There is nothing in the Constitution which actually says who shall be the final arbiter of constitutional questions. There is no express delegation of this authority to the Supreme Court. How the High Court came to wield this awesome power is explainable in terms of the history and tradition of the American legal system, national necessity, and the personalities of some of the outstanding justices.

The delegates to the Philadelphia convention in 1787 ruled that the Constitution would be the "supreme law of the land."

However, they never expressly settled the question of who was to sustain the burden of this supremacy. Alexander Hamilton asserted that this authority should reside in the highest court.

In *The Federalist,* No. 78, Hamilton wrote that the Court had an obligation "to declare all acts contrary to the manifest tenor of the Constitution void." At the same time John Marshall, destined to be one of the greatest justices of the Supreme Court, espoused the theory of judicial review. He announced to the delegates at the ratifying convention in Virginia, "if Congress makes a law not warranted by any of the powers enumerated, it would be considered by the Judges as an infringement of the Constitution which they are to guard. They would not consider such a law coming within their jurisdiction. They would declare it void." This was almost fifteen years before John Marshall officially asserted the doctrine of judicial review in the famous case of *Marbury* v. *Madison.*[1]

Without real debate the First Congress passed the Judiciary Act of 1789, which asserted that the justices of the Supreme Court could refuse to enforce those laws of Congress which they considered to be contrary to the Constitution. In fact, the High Court did review a number of statutes as early as 1794 without invoking cries of outrage. Apparently, the Court also declared a law of Congress invalid at this time.

The election of 1800 voted Jefferson's Republicans into office. Unlike President John Adams and the outgoing Federalist officeholders, the incoming Republicans did not favor the review of legislation by the courts. The Federalists, whose ideas had dominated the Constitutional Convention and who had controlled the national government until 1801, favored judicial review. At this juncture of American history the famous case of

Marbury v. *Madison* came along and forced a confrontation between the Jeffersonians and the Federalists on this issue.

At the end of February, 1801, the lame duck Federalist Congress created a substantial number of new judgeships. Since he was vacating the office of President, John Adams quickly appointed deserving Federalists to these openings. Adams turned over the commissions to John Marshall, his Secretary of State, for the official seals and for delivery. By a momentous quirk of fate, outgoing Secretary of State Marshall had already received his own appointment as new Chief Justice of the Supreme Court. Although Marshall worked into the evening of March 3, 1801, he did not complete the delivery of all the other judicial commissions.

The next day, Thomas Jefferson was sworn in as President of the United States. He ordered that the commissions which had not as yet been delivered should be held up. Marbury, one of the disappointed appointees, sought the assistance of the courts. He invoked Section 13 of the Judiciary Act of 1789 which stated that "in cases warranted" the Supreme Court was permitted to issue a writ of mandamus requiring federal officials to perform routine acts. Marbury asked the Supreme Court to order the new Secretary of State to deliver the commission to him.

John Marshall, the new Chief Justice, was confronted with this dilemma. If the Court issued a writ ordering the delivery of the commission, the recently elected administration would probably ignore it. If the Court did not issue the writ, it would be construed as an admission that the Court had no power over the executive branch; and John Marshall, the new Chief Justice, would be admitting that John Marshall, the old Secretary of State, had committed a serious blunder and, further, that he had been outmaneuvered by Thomas Jefferson and his Republicans.

Marshall's decision was a master stroke. First, he wrote that Marbury was certainly entitled to his commission and that, ordinarily, a proper court could issue a writ of mandamus against a federal official—even a Secretary of State. Then came his twister! He wrote that, although Section 13 of the Judiciary Act purported to give the Supreme Court original jurisdiction to issue such writs, that Section was actually invalid because it was inconsistent with the language of the Constitution. Marshall pointed out that Article III of the Constitution gives the Supreme Court original jurisdiction *only* in those cases which involve ambassadors or other foreign ministers or to which a state is a party. Since Marbury was neither a diplomat or a state, could the Supreme Court enforce a law that was inconsistent with the Constitution? "No," answered Marshall. That ended Marbury's judgeship. And that began the legal authority for the doctrine of judicial review—i.e., the concept that a law which is inconsistent with the Constitution may be declared invalid by the Supreme Court. Marshall explained that the Supreme Court was vested with power to decide the validity of laws in cases actually before the Court. All laws were to be measured against the terms of the Constitution and to be declared void if they did not conform to its requirements.

Marshall's position that an unconstitutional law should not be enforced is unchallengeable. But the question of whether the Supreme Court, rather than the legislature or even the executive, shall make the determination of unconstitutionality, still pops up from time to time. Presidents Jefferson, Jackson, Lincoln, Theodore Roosevelt, and Franklin D. Roosevelt each challenged the doctrine of judicial review. Even today, there is some support for a Court of the Union, which would have authority to overturn the decisions of the Supreme Court. However, to date judicial review is firmly established because Americans generally believe that, to borrow the language used by Justice Robert Jackson in another connection, "One's right to life, liberty and property, to free speech, a free press, freedom of worship and assembly, and other fundamental rights may not be submitted to vote; they depend on the outcome of no elections."[2]

APPLICATION OF THE BILL OF RIGHTS
TO THE STATES

The Bill of Rights was originally intended as a means of restricting the powers of only the national government. However, through interpretation of the Fourteenth Amendment, most of the provisions of the first ten amendments have come to apply also to action by the states. This is one of those feats of legal legerdemain which has deeply touched the life of every American, and it seems fairly clear that this was exactly what the sponsors of the Fourteenth Amendment intended.

Apparently, those who sought the adoption of the first ten amendments felt that they had nothing to fear from their own states because of the safeguards contained in the state constitutions. About sixty-five years later, following the Civil War, the Fourteenth Amendment was adopted. That Amendment provided, in part that no state shall "deprive any person of life, liberty, or property, without due process of law." At least some of the legislative leaders who helped shepherd the Amendment through Congress felt that this provision would apply the Bill of Rights to the states. Nevertheless, in the very first case which arose invoking the Fourteenth Amendment, the High Court ruled that the Bill of Rights was not absorbed into the Fourteenth Amendment in such a way as to restrict the states.[3]

By the turn of the century there had developed substantial sentiment that the federal Bill of Rights should be applied to the states. Even though the constitution of each state contained its own bill of rights, there was feeling that, in many cases, civil liberties were not being protected by the local courts and other law enforcement agencies. In view of the fact that the first ten amendments to the federal Constitution were deemed to apply only against the national government, the Supreme Court could not help persons deprived of their rights by state governments.

Finally, in 1925, there was a breakthrough. In *Gitlow* v. *New York*[4] the right to free speech, as set forth in the First Amendment, was brought within the scope of the "due process of law" provision of the Fourteenth Amendment, thus forcing the states and other local units of government to guarantee this right. All the rights of the first Amendment—free speech and press, freedom of religion, and the right to assemble and petition the government—were brought within the protection of the Due Process Clause of the Fourteenth Amendment by 1937. Thereafter, any act by a local unit of government which allegedly abused these rights could be reviewed on appeal by the Supreme Court of the United States as violative of the United States Constitution. It was even argued that, as a logical progression, any act which would be considered a violation of the federal Bill of Rights, if committed by the federal government, should be considered a violation of the Fourteenth Amendment, if committed by a local government. However, this is a view which most of the justices of the Supreme Court have refused to accept. Instead, the High Court has chosen selectively to enforce some of the rights guaranteed by the first ten amendments and to reject others.

Justice Benjamin N. Cardozo, speaking for the Court in *Palco* v. *Connecticut*,[5] laid down the test for determining which portions of the federal Bill of Rights are to be absorbed into the Due Process Clause of the Fourteenth Amendment so that they also restrict the states. These provisions are the ones dealing with rights "implicit in the concept of ordered liberty"—those which are so fundamental that neither "liberty nor justice would exist if they were sacrificed." As an example, freedom of thought or of expression are so basic that there could be no liberty without them—they are "the matrix, the indispensable condition of nearly every other form of freedom." Conversely, the rights to a jury trial or to indictment by grand jury can be replaced by suitable substitutes and therefore, their loss would not be considered "shocking to the sense of justice of the civilized world."

Using this criterion, the Supreme Court has brought within the limits of the Due Process Clause the First Amendment's guarantees of free speech, free press, religious freedom, and rights to petition and assembly; the Fourth Amendment's protection against unreasonable searches and seizures; the protection against self-incrimination set out in the Fifth Amendment; the right to assistance of counsel and to confront hostile witnesses as provided in the Sixth Amendment; the right to jury trial in criminal cases; and the Eighth Amendment's prohibition against cruel and unusual punishment.

Thus, by the doctrine of judicial review and by selective absorbtion of certain of the first ten amendments into the Fourteenth Amendment, the Supreme Court has been able to maintain a position of extraordinary power over the political, economic, and social life of America.

HOW THE SUPREME COURT DECIDES

Chief Justice Charles Evans Hughes once candidly acknowledged that "the Constitution is what the judges say it is." Why is this so?

The body of the Constitution and its twenty-four amendments can be scanned in a total of about thirty minutes, even without the benefit of a speed reading course. But this superficial reading conveys little of what the Constitution actually means or of how it is applied. Since the turn of the century there have been about two thousand formal proposals to amend the Constitution; yet, to date, only twenty-four of these proposals have actually become amendments.

As Woodrow Wilson once pointed out, the American Constitution in operation is an entirely different thing from the Constitution of the books. In actuality, it is the commentary that the Supreme Court justices have left to us, through their decisions and accompanying opinions, that explains the precise nature of our constitutional system.

It is mistakenly believed by some that the justices of the Supreme Court, like a corps of supermen, have a mission to ferret out the malefactors of America and set things aright. Yet, as has been pointed out, the jurisdiction of the Court is quite circumscribed, and the justices may only exercise the judicial power "to decide and pronounce a judgment and carry it into effect between persons . . . who bring a case before [the Court] for decision." The Court may not intervene unless it is presented with a controversy in actual dispute. In order to have the requisite standing to attack the validity of a statute, the litigant must be "immediately in danger of sustaining a direct injury. It is not sufficient that he has merely a general interest common to all members of the public." The injury must be substantial, not simply a trivial matter.

It is a basic work rule of all judges that they should decide only so much as is absolutely indispensable to dispose of the case under consideration. This approach is especially essential when the judge is faced with an attack on the validity of a statute under the Constitution. As Justice Louis Brandeis once explained, "It is not the habit of the Court to decide questions of a constitutional nature unless absolutely necessary to a decision of a case . . . The Court will not 'formulate a rule of constitutional law broader than is required by the precise facts to which it is to be applied' . . . The Court will not pass upon a constitutional question although properly presented by the record, if there is also present some other ground on which the case may be disposed of . . ."[6]

Thus, the justices do not have unfettered discretion to decide the appeals they review. They are confined by the well worn grooves of legal rules, tradition, and work habits. As Justice Felix Frankfurter once observed, "We do not sit like a kadi under a tree dispensing justice according to considerations of individual expediency. . . . Some of these rules may well appear over-refined or evasive to the laity. But they have the support not only of the profoundest wisdom. They have been vindicated, in conspicuous instances of disregard, by the painful lessons of our constitutional history."[7]

Over the years some of the justices of the Supreme Court have stated from time to time that their function is: simply to find the meaning inherent in the words and phrases of the Constitution, not to impute the meaning they think appropriate. "Judicial power," said Chief Justice John Marshall in 1824, "as contra-distinguished from the power of the States, has no existence. Courts are the mere instruments of the law and can will nothing."[8]

The myth in which the Supreme Court sometimes indulges is that it does not govern or make national policy but, instead, simply expounds on the unchanging and already clear Constitutional document of 1789. The justices have frequently asserted that their job of interpretation or application is simply to find what is already there but clear only to judges and not to the President or the Congress of the United States or to the state courts.

Some of the judges have been more open and have revealed more insight into what is actually going on. For example, in his book, *The Common Law*, Justice Oliver Wendell Holmes once commented, "The felt necessities of the times, the prevalent moral and political feelings, intuitions of public policy, avowed or unconscious, even the prejudices which judges share with their fellow men, have had a good deal more to do than the syllogism in determining the rule by which men should govern." The rest of society has few means of control over the decisions of the Supreme Court. The justices are appointed for life; and, although they may be impeached, impeachment has never been a "scarecrow," as Thomas Jefferson once wryly observed. In spite of a number of other direct and indirect controls, the individual justices of the Supreme Court are about as independent as any person employed by the government in an official capacity can be.

What are the realities of the way the Court works? It may be suspected that some lawsuits have been fictitiously contrived to get a ruling from the Court. Perhaps it is true that, in some instances, the parties have not been exactly adverse.

According to the formal view, a judge is bound by the principle of *stare decisis,* to stand by past precedents and, thus does not actually make law. He simply "discovers" the correct precedents; and, when there is no precise precedent, he merely extends the correct lines of principle.

But this is not as simple as it sounds. The Constitution is a document filled with general phrases such as "due process of law," "cruel and unusual punishment," and "privileges and immunities." There are competing paths of legal precedent as well as many factual differences in each case. Thus, in cases involving the Constitution the justices have considerable leeway in deciding which principle of law to follow. This is also true in cases requiring interpretation or construction of a statute. Many statutes are so inartistically drawn and hurriedly prepared that it is difficult to discover just what the legislature intended. It is not easy for a judge to determine "legislative intent." Even when the statute seems clear, its "plain meaning" may not be so obvious in light of the history of its enactment. As Judge Learned Hand once pointed out, statutory words are "empty vessels into which he [the judge] can pour nearly anything he will."

The justices of the Supreme Court, like the rest of us, do not live in a vacuum. They are influenced by the pressure of social forces, by the economic philosophies they acquired from their upbringing, and by their experience and education.

THE GROWTH OF THE COURT

The birth of the Court and its early history did not augur too well for its future growth. No one was quite sure what the role of the Court should be. It was not easy to find a Chief Justice — as a matter of fact, John Jay, the first Chief Justice, resigned to run for Governor of New York after only five years of service. John Rutledge, who was appointed next, was turned down by the Senate and became insane. The second Chief Justice was Oliver Ellsworth. Because he did not have confidence in the future of the Court and because of poor health, Ellsworth also resigned after five years. With John Marshall, the third Chief Justice, the Supreme Court came into its own. In the next one hundred fifty years, because of the direction pointed by Marshall and the impetus which he initiated, the Court became the pilot boat for the nation's commercial and industrial development, as well as for the federal system. However, by 1937 the High Court had taken a new tack — away from the preoccupation with the preservation and expansion of property values and toward the protection of individual liberty and civil rights.

This change of emphasis was a reaction to the attempt by President Roosevelt to "pack" the Supreme Court. Congress rejected the President's plan to enlarge the Court so that he could be sure of a sympathetic majority; yet even though FDR did not succeed in his packing plan, somehow, a significant change did take place in the attitude of the justices. Thereafter, a concern with freedom for the individual, rather than with the sanctity of property, seemed to be the principal focus of the justices in resolving constitutional issues.

JUDICIAL ACTIVISM VERSUS JUDICIAL PASSIVISM

It is quite clear that the Supreme Court serves as a stabilizer among the three branches of government—legislative, executive, and judicial. The Court resolves major controversies about public policies, both for the states and for the national government. It is the bulwark of authority of the national government with respect to foreign relations. It mediates the continuing friction between majority rule and minority rights, an integral aspect of our dynamic system.

While there are limits to the power of judicial review, these are largely self-inhibitions, imposed by the justices themselves. Not all the judges take the same view of their individual responsibilities in matters of public policy. Although generalizations are not always accurate, it is not unfair to distinguish between the judicial activists, who do not deny that they initiate public policy and explicitly assert their powers as justices of the Court to achieve the social changes they believe imperative, and the other group of justices who believe primarily in self-restraint. The latter group argues that the legislators and the executives elected by the people must bear the burden when it comes to formulating public policy and to adjusting the major competing interests of America. Justice Harlan Stone reflected this viewpoint when he wrote, "Courts are not the only agency of government that must be assumed to have the capacity to govern."[9]

There have been periods in the history of the Supreme Court when the majority has been quite active; and there have been other periods when the majority of the Court has been passive, permitting Congress to take the initiative in areas of policy.

In its philosophy and approach, the Supreme Court has swung back and forth. The Marshall Court asserted national policy confidently and aggressively. For relatively short periods of time—for example, between 1890 and 1936—the justices of the court were restrained by a retarding principle. In the past decade the Supreme Court has taken an active part—perhaps a revolutionary one—in filling what the majority of the justices, under the leadership of Chief Justice Earl Warren, have felt was a vacuum created by the unwillingness of the Congress to meet certain responsibilities under the Constitution. Only time will show the road which the new Chief Justice and his Court will follow.

In such areas as those of racial equality, freedom of speech, suffrage, legislative organization and representation, religious freedom, separation of church and state, immigration and nationality, and the administration of criminal justice, the Court has intervened. It is possible that the tide is receding. It is possible that the administrative difficulties which the High Court faces in enforcing decrees which seek to completely change the pattern of American life are just too much of a burden. However, the willingness of the justices to provide a forum for the hearing of basic complaints against our national and state governments has undoubtedly had a profound effect on American democracy. If there were no such forum within the existing political structure, it is certain that redress would be sought without it—possibly with heavy costs in violence and bloodshed.

In recent years, the Court has shown a marked degree of unanimity on essential issues in spite of some disagreement. Only one justice dissented in the decisions outlawing prayers and Bible reading in the public schools. In the cases concerning racial equality the decisions of the Supreme Court have been virtually unanimous; and, in the cases involving political activities and fair criminal procedures, even when the justices have not agreed, their consensus has been higher than that which existed in the Court during the tumultuous New Deal period. By and large, the dissents have related to specific application rather than to fundamental principle.

Justice Byron R. White has dissented vigorously from several of the decisions that extend the rights of criminal defendants; yet, at the same time, he has defended the Court's active role. At a 1967 conference of state supreme court justices, which met in Hawaii, he said, "I see little reason for the judiciary to apologize for doing as best they can the very job which they are bound to do."

3. Freedom of Religious Conviction

AMENDMENT I

AMERICAN GOVERNMENT and laws have always mirrored a religious society, molded in significant measure by leaders who were convinced that God had placed His hands upon their shoulders. But America has also always been a materialistic society, with only a formal obeisance to spiritual values. The church has traditionally been held apart from the state by a "Wall of Separation." Since colonial days there has been a persistent conflict over the role that religion should play in the life of the country. At the same time, religion has continued to be a deep-seated source of strength and vitality in this nation.

Many of the early settlers fled to these shores to find succor from religious persecution. But religious intolerance, like a noxious weed, quickly took root and flourished in American soil. In many of the original colonies the old victims of persecution established religions of their own dogma and practices, and dissenters from these creeds became the new victims. By the time of the American Revolution, eight colonies had established churches which all their citizens were required to attend, and, in four other colonies, such churches were deemed to be established.[1] Nevertheless, from the very inception of these United States, the idea of a national church has been firmly rejected.

The personality of America has always been strikingly diverse and pluralistic. But it has been most fecund and astonishingly variegated in its proliferation of religious creeds. Perhaps, as James Madison pointed out at the Virginia Convention of 1788, freedom of religion in America "arises from the multiplicity of sects which pervade America and which is the best and only security for religious liberty in any society." Certainly the competition of the numerous religious groups and denominations has served as a sturdy floodgate, holding back the strong tides of religious intolerance.

As an early order of business, the First Congress gave serious consideration to formulating a proposal protecting freedom of religious conviction. After a number of language changes, the Rights of Conscience Clause was finally worded as it reads in the opening portion of the First Amendment:

> Congress shall make no law respecting an establishment of religion, or prohibiting the free exercise thereof.

Since this provision explicitly restricted its prohibition only to the federal Congress, the individual states were still free to establish their particular religions. As a consequence, for many years, various states favored specific religions and maintained religious qualifications for voting and holding office. However, in 1940 it was finally decided that the First Amendment limits the states as well as the federal government.[2] The law is now clear—the Fourteenth Amendment serves to insure that a state may not adopt laws "respecting an establishment of religion, or prohibiting the free exercise thereof." It is noteworthy that there are two different restrictions imposed by the Constitution. One forbids the establishment of religion; the other forbids prohibiting the free exercise of religion. Although these guarantees overlap, each presents certain unique distinctions.

ESTABLISHMENT OF RELIGION

During the early days of the Republic, Thomas Jefferson, in a phrase time-honored by judicial usage, advanced the idea that the First Amendment serves as a "Wall of Separation" between church and state. The Supreme Court has maintained that the government should be religiously neutral and has explained its position in these terms:

> The "establishment of religion" clause of the First Amendment means at least this: Neither a state nor the Federal Government can set up a church. Neither can pass laws which aid one religion, aid all religions, or prefer one religion over another. Neither can force nor influence a person to go to or to remain away from church against his will or force him to profess a belief or disbelief in any religion. No person can be punished for entertaining or professing religious belief or disbeliefs; for church attendance or non-attendance.[3]

There are no cases which deal directly with an attempt, either by Congress or a state legislature, to recognize an official church. Nevertheless, there have been a number of cases which dealt with the question of whether or not the government did, in effect, establish a religion, if not a specific church. For example, Maryland's attempt to require all persons applying for a notary public commission to sign a statement that they believed in a Supreme Being was held to violate the First Amendment.[4] The Court ruled that such a requirement breaches the obligation of the government to be neutral in matters of religion, since it might coerce the applicant into stating a belief not in accordance with his conscience.

The Establishment Clause has been central in a number of recent civil rights controversies. Some of these have dealt with the church-state problem in the field of education. Others have related to the laws requiring stores to close on Sunday.

Religious Freedom and Education

The First Amendment was the foundation for a 1923 decision which set aside a Nebraska law forbidding teachers in Lutheran schools and their pupils to engage in religious activities conducted in the German language. Two years later an Oregon law requiring most children between eight and sixteen years of age to attend public schools was also declared unconstitutional. These cases upheld the free exercise of religion within church-related schools and paved the way for the First Amendment cases to come.

The Establishment Clause has been held to prevent the use of tax funds by church-related educational institutions. Justice Black gave voice to this restriction in the case of *Everson* v. *Board of Education.*[5]

> No tax in any amount, large or small, can be levied to support any religious activities or institutions, whatever they may be called, or whatever form they may adopt to teach or practice religion. Neither a state nor the Federal Government can, openly or secretly, participate in the affairs of any religious organizations or groups and vice versa.

In the Everson case it was decided that, for reasons of public safety, a school board in New Jersey could use tax funds to reimburse parents for bus fares paid to transport pupils to and from their parochial schools. However, all the justices agreed with the philosophy of the Establishment Clause as formulated by Justice Black. The Supreme Court, shortly thereafter, indicated that public school facilities cannot be made available to clergymen during school time for purposes of providing religious instruction for the children who wish to receive it.[6] However, it is legal to release children from their public school classes so that they may receive religious training at some other place.[7] In 1962 it was decided that the Board of Regents of the State of New York could not write a prayer to be used in public schools, even if the pupils who found it objectionable were allowed to be excused.[8] And a year later the Court held that Pennsylvania and Baltimore could not require that the Lord's Prayer be recited or portions of the Bible read in the public schools.[9] Not too long ago, pupils in a certain public school kindergarten were required to recite the following before their morning snack:

> We thank you for the flowers so sweet;
> We thank you for the food we eat;
> We thank you for the birds that sing;
> We thank you for everything.

This was regarded as a prayer, and its compulsory recital was said to violate the constitutional proscription against the establishment of religion.[10]

The so-called Blaine Amendment of the New York State Constitution specifically bans aid to church-supported schools.[11] This issue has been held responsible by many for the defeat of a proposed constitution which would have eliminated this Amendment and, thus, permitted such assistance. In an address before the New York State Legislature on January 8, 1968, Bishop Fulton J. Sheen, of Rochester, alluded indirectly to this issue. He said, "I am happy that though our children can't pray in the classroom, we can still pray in our legislature—if we wish to keep our rights and liberties, we have to keep our God."

In *Abington Township School District* v. *Schempp*,[12] the High Court set forth the following test to be used in church-education cases: If the essential purpose of a law either advances or inhibits religion, then it is not within the constitutional authority of a legislature. Unfortunately, it is easier to state a principle then to apply it to a concrete set of facts.

In 1967 a New York housewife, Florence Flast, and a number of other taxpayers initiated a suit in the federal court. They argued that their taxes were being illegally spent when distributed through federal aid to education, which paid for tutoring in parochial schools. The lower court never decided the substantive claim because the case was dismissed for lack of "standing." The court felt that, as ordinary taxpayers, the plaintiffs did not have a sufficient legal stake in the constitutional issue to justify their bringing a lawsuit. Their interest was considered too minuscule to support a suit which was based on the argument that a specific federal expenditure exceeded the general legislative powers of Congress.

When the dispute reached the Supreme Court,[13] the majority, by an eight to one decision, ruled in Mrs. Flast's favor—saying that her interest in the issue at hand was great enough to permit her to bring a lawsuit.

At this time the Court enunciated a new rule for determining whether a person who initiates a lawsuit has sufficient "standing" to sue. The taxpayer who feels he is so "aggrieved" that he has the right to sue must show that the statute under attack "exceeds specific constitutional limitations imposed upon the exercise of congressional taxing and spending power." In the Flast case the majority did not specify which congressional limitations it had in mind. But, in a concurring opinion, Justice Fortas made the strong contention that only the Establishment of Religion Clause could serve as a basis for an action.

At the same time, in another case,[14] the Supreme Court decided the question of whether New York, or any other state, can require local school boards to loan textbooks to pupils in private schools, including those schools with church affiliation. The school boards of two New York counties contended that the state law authorizing such programs was a violation of the First Amendment's ban upon the establishment of religion. The Court ruled that such assistance was proper on the theory that the primary objective of the New York law was to help children, rather than to promote the interests of religion.

The majority opinion, expressed by Justice White, relied heavily on a case, decided a decade earlier, in which the Court had ruled that the states could reimburse parents for the cost of bussing their children to parochial schools. However, in the textbook case, the three dissenters, Justices Douglas, Fortas, and Black, pointed out that many books, ostensibly secular, may be religious in their treatment of such subjects as evolution. Said Black:

> It requires no pamphlet to foresee that on the argument used to support the law, others could be upheld providing for funds to buy property on which to erect religious school buildings, to pay the salaries of religious school teachers, and finally to pick up all the bills for religious schools. I still subscribe to the belief that tax-raised funds cannot constitutionally be used to support religious schools, even to the extent of one penny.

There is considerable disagreement as to the ultimate impact of these two cases. Dr. Leo Pfeffer, professor of law at Long Island University, has predicted an "era of litigation" likely to reinforce the separation of church and state. He has stated, "there will be many cases reaching the Court before fairly definite guidelines on the constitutionality of government aid to church-sponsored schools are worked out."[15]

Many experts feel that these two cases have very broad implications. Dr. Marvin Schick, professor of political science at Hunter College, feels that the Court has "clearly proclaimed that parochial schools serve the public interest and provide essential public service."[16] He has said that the time has now come when we must recognize that it is the obligation of government, at all levels, to afford teaching aids and special educational programs, such as reading and guidance, for parochial schools.

Sunday Compulsory Store Closing Laws

In May, 1961, the United States Supreme Court handed down decisions in four cases sustaining the validity of Sunday closing laws in Maryland, Massachusetts, and Pennsylvania. The Court held that it was not a violation of the Constitution for a state to designate Sunday as a *secular* day of rest, although, originally, Sunday closing laws were enacted to promote the observance of the Sabbath—certainly a religious concept. The logic of the opinion, as stated in one of the cases, was that, since the underlying reason for the law was no longer religious, it did not run afoul of the First Amendment.[17]

Nevertheless, some fifteen states have exemptions in favor of persons who, for reasons of religious convictions, keep their stores closed on days other than Sunday. Ironically, since the Sunday compulsory store closing decisions, questions have been raised as to whether an exemption is not itself unconstitutional on the ground that it is an aid to religion, and, thus, is discriminatory. These exemptions have been accused of violating the Fourteenth Amendment's guarantee of equal protection of the laws in that they grant a preference to religion by excusing those of a particular faith from an obligation imposed on everyone else.

One alternative accepted by some states is the weekend closing law. This law gives every storekeeper the option of keeping his business closed regularly, either on Saturday or on Sunday, and there is no need for a special motivation to exercise this alternative. The owner may act out of religious conviction or out of the economic conviction that one day, rather than the other, will be more profitable. So far only two states have passed weekend closing laws—Texas, in 1961, and Michigan, in 1962. However, the idea may be adopted by more states because it avoids the problem of prying into a storekeeper's religious convictions and it seems to avoid the constitutional hurdle.

FREE EXERCISE OF RELIGION

The Establishment Clause requires that government do nothing to take away a man's belief—it must be neutral toward religion. The Free Exercise Clause protects a man's right to act in accordance with his religious convictions, but this is not an unlimited right—it is subject to control by government.

First, it must be understood that, under the decisions of the Supreme Court, the term "religion" in the First Amendment comprehends the right to believe, as well as the right to disbelieve, in accordance with one's conscience. However, there is a tremendous difference between belief and disbelief, on one hand, and action predicated upon these convictions, on the other hand. Government may not control a man's belief, but it may control his acts. For example, a Mormon has an absolute right to believe that God has ordained that he have as many wives as possible. Yet, under the Free Exercise Clause, he does not have a right to carry out God's mandate.[18] While an individual has the right, under the Free Exercise Clause, to practice his religion according to his conscience, so long as his acts do not harm others or the community as a whole, the government may restrict him in his religious practices if his acts violate his obligations to society or if they may cause injury to society.

A number of problems under the First Amendment illustrate how the Free Exercise of Religion Clause works. They all involve the right to freedom of conscience, and they also point up how the Establishment Clause and the Free Exercise Clause of the First Amendment relate to each other.

The Flag Salute Cases

The issue of the extent to which a man may freely exercise his religious beliefs is illustrated most ghaphically by the litigation involving the defiance of Jehovah's Witnesses toward statutes making it compulsory to salute the flag. About a quarter of a century ago the West Virginia Board of Education ordered that pupils who refused to salute the flag were to be expelled from school. This came to pass when parents, who happened to be Jehovah's Witnesses, directed their children not to take part in the "pledge allegiance to the flag" ceremony. Ultimately, the case of one of the contumacious pupils reached the Supreme Court of the United States.[19] In a six to three decision, the Court, speaking through Justice Robert H. Jackson, decided:

> . . . action of the local authorities in compelling the flag salute and pledge transcends constitutional limitations on their power and involves the sphere of intellect and spirit which it is the purpose of the First Amendment to reserve from all official control. . . .
>
> Freedom to differ is not limited to things that do not matter much. That would be a mere shadow of freedom. The test of its substance is the right to differ as to things that touch the heart of the existing order.
>
> If there is any fixed star in our constitutional constellation, it is that no official, high or petty, can prescribe what shall be orthodox in politics, nationalism, religion, or other matters of opinion or force citizens to confess by word or act of faith. . . .

In another case[20] decided the very same day, the Supreme Court reinforced its position by invalidating a Mississippi statute which made it illegal to urge people not to salute the flag for religious reasons.

It is ironic that, only three years before, the Supreme Court had espoused a diagonally opposite approach to this proposition. A flag salute case[21] had come before the court in 1940 from another state. All but one of the justices had refused to sanction religious protest to the flag salute. The sole dissenter was Justice Harlan Stone, who observed: "History teaches us that there have been but few infringements of personal liberty by the state, which have not been justified, as they are here, in the name of righteousness and the public good, and few which have not been directed, as they are now, at politically helpless minorities . . ."

The Right to Propagate the Faith

There are many cases which deal with public proselytizing by various religious groups. It is difficult to reconcile the holdings of these cases, which involve application of the principles of free speech, religious freedom, and the right of assembly, on one hand, and the need of the organized community to maintain order and protect the rest of the population in its right to be free from intrusion, on the other hand.

Certain specific rights have been established. A person may give out religious tracts on the streets and other public places without prior permission from any public officials.[22] He may even distribute such literature in a privately owned town without the owner's permission or in a federally owned housing project. He may play phonograph records for any person who is willing to listen to religious propaganda. He may push religious tracts. He may solicit funds for a religious cause without a permit or payment of a license fee, even though he makes his living exclusively from the sale of religious books.

In connection with the holding of religious meetings in public parks, no religious sect may be discriminated against because of its religious beliefs. Nor may a state vest a police officer with unrestrained authority to grant or deny permits to speak on religious subjects in public places. Furthermore, a minister who has been denied a permit under such conditions may not be punished for preaching without a permit.

On the other hand, a number of restrictions on the exercise of religion have been upheld by the Court. A city ordinance regulating the use of streets for religious parades and imposing a reasonable discretionary fee for the cost of the administration of parades is valid.[23] A state statute forbidding the address of offensive and derisive language to anyone who is lawfully in the street or in some other public place is also valid.[24] The state Child Labor Laws may be validly applied to those who permit children under their care to sell religious literature on the streets. A person may be constitutionally punished for holding a religious meeting in a public park without a permit required by local ordinance, even though he has properly sought the permit and has been arbitrarily and legally refused by those responsible for administering the ordinance—providing that the state permits a judicial remedy for such arbitrary refusal.[25]

Conscientious Objectors and the Refusal to Bear Arms

When James Madison, at the request of Congress, drafted a Bill of Rights for the newly adopted Constitution, he proposed, "No person religiously scrupulous shall be compelled to render military service in person." Although this proposal was rejected in Congress, it was adopted in some state constitutions. For example, the New York Constitution of 1821 provided that "all such inhabitants of this state, of any religious denomination whatever, as from scruples of conscience may be averse to bearing arms, shall be excused therefrom by paying to the state an equivalent in money." The first national conscription act, adopted in 1863, specifically exempted the Quakers, but the following year it was amended to exclude all "members of religious denominations who shall by oath or affirmation declare that they are conscientiously opposed to the bearing of arms, and who are prohibited from doing so by the rules and articles of faith and practice of said religious denominations."

While the 1864 amendment extended the exemption to sects other than the Quakers, it did require membership in a specific pacifist denomination. This requirement was continued in the draft law enacted in 1917 at the outbreak of World War I. The exemption was likewise limited to members of "well recognized" religious sects whose creeds or principles forbade participation in war.

By 1940 American concepts of religious individualism had broadened, and the Selective Service Act adopted that year eliminated the requirement of membership in a "well recognized" sect. It was sufficient for exemption that the applicant by "reason of religious training and belief" possessed conscientious scruples against "participation in war in any form." In

1948, however, Congress made it clear that it did not intend to exempt those who objected to participation in war on grounds other than religion, and that its concept of "religion" was based on a belief in God. The 1948 amendment stated that religion "means an individual's belief in a relation to a Supreme Being involving duties superior to those arising from any human relation, but does not include essentially political, sociological, or philosophical views or a merely personal moral code."

The 1917 draft act was challenged in the courts,[26] primarily on the ground that it violated the Thirteenth Amendment's ban on involuntary servitude. However, an incidental basis for attack was that its exemption of religious objectors and clergymen constituted a law respecting an establishment of religion in violation of the First Amendment. The Supreme Court rejected this claim as being so untenable that it did not even require the justices to detail the reasons for the rejection.

But if, as this case held, the Establishment Clause of the First Amendment does not forbid exemption of conscientious objectors, neither does the Free Exercise Clause require it. This would seem to follow necessarily from the fact that Madison's proposal to write an exemption into the Bill of Rights was defeated. In any event, the Court has consistently so held. In *Hamilton* v. *Regents of California*[27] it was ruled that a state university could constitutionally expel students who, on religious grounds, refused to take military training. In the case *In re Summers*,[28] it held that a state could bar conscientious objectors from practicing law, and, in *United States* v. *MacIntosh*,[29] it held that Congress has the power to bar them from naturalization. (The present nautralization law expressly exempts religious pacifists from the oath to bear arms.) The reason for these decisions is that national defense is so important that it must override any claim to religious freedom.

The major task of the courts therefore has, until recently, been to interpret and apply the exemption from military service granted by Congress to conscientious objectors, rather than to pass on its constitutionality. Typical of such interpretive cases is *Sicurella* v. *United States*[30] in which the Court held that a Jehovah's Witness could not "be denied the benefits of the exemption simply because the writings of the sect extol the ancient wars of the Israelites" and state that Witnesses would fight at Armageddon. "As to theocratic wars," the Court said, "petitioner's willingness to fight on the orders of Jehovah is tempered by the fact that, so far as we know, their history records no such command since Biblical times and their theology does not appear to contemplate one in the future."

The war in Vietnam has raised a significant civil liberties concept—selective conscientious objection. Traditionally, the claim of the conscientious objector has been based upon adherence to a recognized religion. But, in a landmark case, the Supreme Court has gone beyond this point. In *United States* v. *Seeger*[31] the justices were forced to decide whether a man, who calls himself a conscientious objector and says that his "religious training and belief" prevents him from participating in a war, can be exempt from military service even though he is not a member of a traditionally recognized pacifistic religious denomination. The Court ruled that the clause of the Selective Service Law which exempts conscientious objectors can be interpreted so as to comprehend a wide spectrum of religious expression, including the beliefs of people who have not found any traditional church which satisfies their needs. The objector has only to possess beliefs which forbid his participation in all wars and which "occupy the same place in his life as the belief in a traditional diety."

The issue of objection to a specific war raises the spectre of the judgments rendered at Nuremberg against German war criminals. The underlying reason for these judgments was the thesis that each person must decide for himself the morality and legality of the acts of his country and refuse to obey orders which would force him to commit a crime against humanity.

This doctrine has been raised in connection with the Vietnam

War. A noteworthy example is the case of Captain Howard B. Levy, who was court-martialed for his refusal to train Green Berets in certain medical practices. While the military tribunal did admit evidence based upon the theory of the Nuremberg trials, this defense has not yet been recognized in the civil courts.[32]

Cassius Clay, or Muhammad Ali, has denounced his conviction for refusing to be drafted, charging that a "lily white" draft board had unconstitutionally denied him a religious exemption. He had sought an exemption from the draft as a Black Muslim minister. However, a series of local draft boards and appeals boards within the Selective Service System refused to change his 1-A classification.[33]

On January 5, 1968, Dr. Benjamin Spock and four other men were indicted for conspiring to persuade young men to violate the draft laws. The defendants made no attempt to conceal their antidraft sentiments or activities. Some of them said that they were deliberately violating the law, as a form of antiwar protest. When one of the defendants, Yale Chaplain William Sloane Coffin, Jr., left a batch of draft protestors' selective service cards at the Justice Department in the fall of 1967, he demanded a "moral, legal confrontation" with the government over the war. Spock and the other defendants were convicted.

Initially, some of the defendants literally insisted on being prosecuted. None of them hid the fact that they were engaged in civil disobedience by violating the edicts of the Selective Service Act. The defendants were charged with having collected draft cards and returning them to the government. The prosecution said this was criminal because draft registrants are required to carry their cards at all times.

The defendants took the position that they could not be held accountable for opposing a war that was itself illegal. But the trial judge, even before the trial began, eliminated the important issue of the legality of the Vietnam War. All that was left then was a defense based on the right of free speech. The defendants' lawyer argued that the return of the cards was "symbolic speech," a harmless gesture from the conscience, insignificant except as an expression of opposition to the war. The lower court convicted the five men, but this does not appear to have resolved any of the underlying problems, legal or ethical, which the refusal to bear arms raises.[34]

To date, the landmark precedent for these convictions is the *Schenk* v. *United States*[35] decision of 1919. In that case the defendants had been convicted for mailing circulars to draftees, urging them to resist induction. Writing for a unanimous Court, Justice Holmes had ruled that the First Amendment did not protect Schenk because there was a "clear and present danger" that his circulars would persuade draftees to break the law.

4. Freedom of Expression

AMENDMENT I

FREEDOM OF THOUGHT is an old idea but scarcely an old-fashioned one. However, thought alone, without communication, is analogous to the lost Bedouin, parched with thirst, sinking all alone into the desert sands, shouting for water to the searing, impersonal, unresponsive sun. Thought acquires social value only when it is transmitted to someone capable of responding to it. Thus, freedom of expression must go hand-in-hand with freedom of thought before there can be social progress.

In view of the fact that the Declaration of Independence emphasized the pursuit of individual happiness as a significant democratic goal, perhaps freedom of expression can be justified on the simple thesis that it is a mode of self-realization for man —the social creature. However, there are other far more impressive reasons for cherishing the right to freedom of expression.

There are two major rationales which buttress the importance of free discussion. Informed public opinion, developed through an open exchange of views among the citizenry, is the best check on the officials of a democratic government. Thomas Jefferson wrote a friend that, if the people once "become inattentive to public affairs, you and I, and Congress and assemblies, judges and governors, shall all become wolves." The other argument in favor of free discussion is that the greatest chance of finding solutions to the problems which plague the community lies in intercourse of ideas and proposals between those most concerned. As a great jurist once observed, the public good is most usually "reached by free trade in ideas... the best test of truth is the power of thought to get itself accepted in the competition of the market."[1]

Certainly, without the efforts of such patriotic speakers and pamphleteers as James Otis, Patrick Henry, Thomas Paine, and the zealous Committees of Correspondence proselytizing for the cause of independence, the American nation would not have come into existence. Mindful of this revolutionary experience and bolstered by the theories of Locke and Montesquieu with respect to self-government, the leading draftsmen of the Constitution made certain that one of the first guarantees set out in the Bill of Rights was that contained in the First Amendment:

> Congress shall make no law... abridging the freedom of speech, or of the press.

By its express terms this provision restricted only action by Congress. However, since 1925, through the Fourteenth Amendment, this guarantee has served to forbid the states from curtailing or denying freedom of speech or press.[2]

Freedom of expression usually brings to mind the dissemination of ideas through oral communication and through written language. Of course, speech and writing have never been the only methods of human expression. Humans have always communicated non-verbally through various types of action and through facial and bodily movement. The medium of expression and the message are inextricably related, as Marshall McLuhan has pointed out, and science continues to surprise us with new techniques for communication.

The First Amendment casts its protective shield over all sorts of ideas and their communication. Thus, radio, television, cinema, and photographs are all included. Not only written and spoken language, but also pictures unaccompanied by sound are protected by the Constitution.[3] The decisions of the Supreme Court assert that free speech includes "appropriate types of action," as well as verbal expression. Among the varieties of symbolic expression protected by the High Court are the refusal of Jehovah's Witness children to salute the American flag, the display of a red flag by protestors as a sign of disapproval of government action, and peaceful picketing and demonstration.

LIMITS ON FREEDOM OF EXPRESSION

The language of the First Amendment comes through loud and clear. It trumpets a guarantee of free speech and press in unequivocal terms. Yet, irresponsibly employed words may incite a mob to homicidal rampage. The false shout of "fire" may unleash panic in a crowded hall, or a lie about some ethnic or religious group may tear assunder the tranquility of a somnolent community. Therefore, while everyone is in favor of free speech, no nation on the face of the earth has permitted unbridled freedom of expression. Even in America, the courts have found it necessary to strike a balance between the bold black letter assurance that Congress shall not abridge freedom of speech or of the press and the social needs which create pressures for control of freedom of expression. Only a few judges, notably Justice Hugo Black of the Supreme Court, have subscribed to the view that the only limits which should be imposed on free speech are the sound judgments of the community since "these are safer corrections than the conscience of the judge."

In 1798, a scant seven years after the First Amendment was adopted, the Federalists jammed the Alien and Sedition Acts through Congress. These laws were passed to meet an alleged conspiracy against the United States fomented by *agents provocateurs* of France. In the ensuing hysteria innocent citizens were clapped into jail for criticizing President John Adams;

outspoken newspapermen were imprisoned for "subversive" articles and editorials; Frenchmen, long-time residents in this country, were deported. In his campaign for the presidency Thomas Jefferson used this issue as ammunition; and, after Jefferson was elected, in 1806 the Alien and Sedition Laws came to an end.

The "Clear and Present Danger" Test

These laws never came before the Supreme Court for review. As a matter of record, it was only after World War I that, as a result of prosecutions brought under the Espionage Act of 1917 and the Sedition Act of 1918, the High Court was confronted with appeals which tested the limits of free speech in time of national crisis. In response to one of these appeals, the Court sustained the application of the Espionage Act of 1917 to an officer of the Socialist party named Schenk. He had distributed anti-draft leaflets during the war to men who were subject to service in the armed forces. In passionate and inflammatory language, the pamphlets had urged men to resist the draft. It was Justice Holmes who formulated the yardstick to be applied by the Supreme Court in such cases. He stated:

> The question in every case is whether the words are used in such circumstances and are of such nature as to create a clear and present danger that they bring about the substantial evil that Congress has a right to prevent. It is a question of proximity and degree. When a nation is at war many things that might be said at a time of peace are such a hindrance to its effort that their utterance will not be endured as long as men fight, and no court can regard them as protected by a Constitutional right.[4]

The appropriateness of this test was also studied in another epochal case about the same time. The Abram's case,[5] upheld the application of the Sedition Act of 1918 to a person who distributed Marxist leaflets which urged "Workers of the World" to resist the intervention of the Allies, including the Americans, against the Bolshevik forces following the Russian Revolution. Justices Holmes and Brandeis dissented. They contended that "clear and present danger" had been shown. Wrote Holmes:

> I think that we should be eternally vigilant against the attempts to check the expression of opinions that we loathe and believe to be fraught with danger, unless they so imminently threaten immediate interference with the lawful and present purposes of the law that an immediate check is required to save the country.

Another conviction for the publication of articles attacking the war effort was sustained,[6] as was one based upon a speech attacking America's participation in World War I.[7] The judges were not always unanimous in use of the "clear and present danger" doctrine, nor were they always consistent in applying the concept to specific situations.[8] It was not until 1937 that the "clear and present danger" test finally gained acceptance by the entire Court.[9]

The "Bad Tendency" Test

In 1925 the Supreme Court formulated a new test which limited free speech far more than did the "clear and present danger" approach which had been used before. In *Gitlow* v. *New York*,[10] the majority of the Court upheld the New York Criminal Anarchy Syndicalism Act as applied to the publication of a left-wing manifesto which asserted that our society could be saved from the evils of capitalism "only by the Communist Revolution." Even though the publication and, in addition, various speeches did not constitute a "clear and present danger," the Court decided that the state legislature could declare acts criminal even if they had only a "tendency" to bring about such results—that "It was enough if the natural tendency and probable effect was to bring about the substantive evils which the legislative body might prevent." It was much easier to restrict free speech under this rule than under the "clear and present danger" test.

Although the "bad tendency" test was invoked in a few cases, by 1937 the Supreme Court had returned to the "clear and present danger" test as enunciated by Justice Holmes.

The "Preferred Position" Test

In a now famous footnote, Justice Harlan Stone observed that it seems fairly basic to the principles of constitutional democracy that legislation which restricts political processes should be subjected "to more exacting judicial scrutiny under the general prohibition of the Fourteenth Amendment than are most other types of legislation."[11] This was an extension of Justice Benjamin N. Cardozo's statement that the freedoms of the First Amendment are the fountainhead of virtually all other freedoms, and, for this reason, it is appropriate for the Supreme Court to invoke a more rigorous standard of review in cases concerned with these freedoms than in other cases arising under the Constitution.[12]

In a number of appeals decided in the 1940's, the doctrine of the "preferred status" of the First Amendment's freedoms became the basis of a rejuvenated "clear and present danger" approach. For instance, in one review the Court stated that the First Amendment's freedoms enjoy a "preferred position" and, therefore, any attempt to restrict these freedoms must be scrutinized carefully.[13]

Not all the justices have accepted the "preferred position" for free speech, but the High Court has, in effect, continued to use the test of "clear and present danger." This does not mean, however, that the Court has always reached consistent results. Compare, as an illustration, *Terminiello* v. *Chicago*,[14] with *Feiner* v. *New York*.[15] In the Terminiello case the Court did not find a "clear and present danger" in an anti-Semitic harangue.

although the bitter words did cause a riot. Yet, in the Feiner case, which involved a certain speech intended to incite Negro people against whites, the conviction was upheld, although no violence had taken place.

Other Judicial Tests

The Supreme Court has employed other tests besides the ones just discussed. One of these is the "sliding scale" test, which involves careful evaluation of the facts of each individual case in order to determine whether the danger inherent in a particular situation is great enough to warrant curtailment of any of the freedoms of the First Amendment. Two cases provide apt examples.

Dennis v. *United States*[16] involved the validity of the first peacetime sedition law to be passed by Congress since the Sedition Act of 1798. This piece of legislation, commonly known as the Smith Act, was the Alien Registration Act of 1940. It was a major weapon in the prosecution of American Communist party leaders by the federal government. The Court upheld the conviction of eleven top Communist functionaries and the validity of the Smith Act. While the opinion was couched in terms of the old "clear and present danger" test, it actually employed the "sliding scale," which the lower court judge had used. The majority explained that it had come to its decision only after asking "whether the gravity of the 'evil' discounted by its improbability, justifies such erosion of free speech as is necessary to avoid the danger."[17]

Still another case[18] involved a situation in which the economic theories of Marxism and Communism had been advocated but there had apparently been no actual incitement to violence or advocacy that this government be overthrown by violent revolution either now or in the future. In this case the Court refused to sustain the convictions of all the defendants under the Smith

Act. However, it did sustain the convictions of those defendants who belonged to the Communist party and who knew that the Communist party urged the overthrow of this government, by force if necessary.

Another factor which the Court has apparently considered important in determining whether a speech constitutes a danger is the state of mind of the speaker. It appears that the Supreme Court has been more ready to sustain a conviction if the person involved clearly intended to bring about the substantive evil his ideas expressed. At times, the Court has combined "evil intent" of the speaker with the "bad tendency" of the speech or with the test of a "clear and present danger." At other times, the Court has relied heavily on the factor of "evil intent" alone. It is thus difficult to evaluate exactly how much influence the "evil intent" will have on the Court, but it usually will be recognized as a factor.

In the Gitlow case[19] the Court punished the person uttering the words having a "bad tendency" and expressed with an "evil intent." In *Whitney* v. *California*,[20] Justice Brandeis asserted the "clear and present danger" test so as to include intention to create such danger. In *Fiske* v. *Kansas*[21] the Supreme Court set aside the conviction of an Industrial Workers of the World organizer under the Anti-Syndicalism Law of Kansas because it had not been shown that the defendant had ever intended to bring about his industrial and political goals by violence or other unlawful means. In the Yates case,[22] the Court went one step further and decided that advocacy of the violent overthrow of government, even with intention to bring about this result, could not be punished under the Smith Act unless the language employed was likely to incite violence.

In summation, it seems as if the High Court has fixed the limits of free speech by taking into account both the results which the ideas will probably bring about and the intrinsic nature of the ideas themselves—there has been a balancing of the ideas and the likely result. In general, if the ideas expressed are very dangerous, the Court is not likely to insist on proof that an immediate and dangerous consequence is imminent. If the ideas are not very dangerous intrinsically, the Court is likely to insist on its being clearly shown that a dangerous consequence is imminent.

OBSCENITY

The Supreme Court has been wrestling for some time with the problem of speech and literature which deviate from the current moral standards of the community, which shock or offend readers, or which stimulate sexual thoughts or desires. The Court tried to avoid this problem by neatly declaring that obscenity is not protected by the First Amendment. Alas, this fiat neither made the problem vanish nor met it head on. It is one thing to pop a legal issue under a nutshell; it is another thing to keep it there.

In 1957, after enunciating the principle that the free speech guarantee of the First Amendment does not protect obscene material, the Supreme Court began the task of turning over slimy rocks to unearth obscenity. And then, the justices fell to squabbling over just what "obscene" means. Obscenity, like beauty, is largely in the eyes of the beholder. The usual local obscenity laws make it a crime for persons to peddle such things as magazines, books, films, and live performances that are obscene, lewd, filthy, lascivious, or immoral. Since one man's meat is another man's poison, different people construe these words in different ways. The words do not tell the bookdealer, the jurist, or the policeman where to draw the line between innocent sex and criminal pornography.

For the past decade the Supreme Court has been stirring a bouillabaisse of steaming cases dealing with the question of what is obscene. It has been said that, even though a specific play or book may contain four letter words or explicit descriptions of sexual acts, this does not mean that the work will be automatically adjudged obscene, provided that the material taken as a whole is of some literary value or importance to society. Works which have no literary value or social importance, but are hard-core pornography or filth for its own sake, are considered obscene.

In *Roth* v. *United States*,[23] the High Court suggested that the test for obscenity is "whether to the average person, applying contemporary community standards, the dominant theme of the material taken as a whole appeals to the prurient interest." The dominant theme of a work—not simply a few sentences or a single paragraph taken alone—is the yardstick. Furthermore, the values of only one individual cannot be the basis for condemning a literary work, the standard must be the "common conscience of the community."[24]

The Supreme Court has also warned that the effect of a work on a narrow segment of society cannot be the basis for determining obscenity. If a work is not obscene by the standards of adults, it is not metamorphosed into an obscene book just because it might appeal to the prurient interest of an adolescent.[25] A work cannot be barred from publication or sale because it might titillate a diseased mind. The contents must be both patently offensive and appealing to the prurient interest of the average man, according to Justice Harlan.[26]

With little fanfare, on May 8, 1967, in a case called *Redrup* v. *New York*,[27] the Supreme Court quietly issued an unsigned opinion which threw out a batch of obscenity appeals that had been argued on highly technical grounds. The opinion did not set forth specific reasons for the decision. However, it did mention three elements that did not appear in the cases which were dismissed: No case involved an obscenity law directed expressly toward protection of youngsters; no case presented an "assault" on the public by a display of pornography; and no case involved the "pandering" of spicy wares.

The Redrup case seems to reflect those areas in which the

Supreme Court feels intervention by law is warranted. In April, 1968, by a vote of six to three, the Court ruled that states may make it a crime to knowingly sell "to minors under seventeen years of age, material described as obscene to youngsters whether or not it would be obscene to grownups."[28]

In 1965 a teenage boy purchased a couple of pinup picture magazines from a local luncheonette and stationery store. Sam Ginsberg, the proprietor, was convicted under the newly passed New York law forbidding sale of obscene material to juveniles, and he appealed his conviction. His lawyers argued that the right of an individual to read or look at publications "cannot be made to depend on whether the citizen is an adult or a minor." Justice William Brennan, speaking for the majority, pointed out that "the well-being of its children is of course a subject within the state's constitutional power to regulate." He conceded that it has not been scientifically established, as yet, that such material actually impairs, in the words of the New York law, the "ethical and moral development of youth." But, since the Court does not require that legislatures have "scientifically certain criteria for legislation," it could not rule that the New York law "has no rational relation to the objective of safeguarding minors from harm."

In his dissent, Justice Fortas noted that the youth had been sent to buy the girlie magazines by his mother, who wished to put Ginsberg out of business. Fortas added, "Bookselling should not be a hazardous profession."

Recently, the Supreme Court let stand the conviction of a Miami sculptor who offered for sale in his yard life-sized statues of couples in assorted imaginative erotic embraces—figures which probably would not have been considered obscene if they had been discretely offered for sale.[29] Even those who agree with Justices Hugo L. Black and William O. Douglas that all erotic expression should be protected by the Constitution think that the public should be spared the nuisance of visual assaults by pornographic displays. The problem of the "pandering" of smut, as mentioned in the Redrup opinion, was before the Court in 1966, when the justices upheld the conviction of Ralph Ginzburg, publisher of, among other things, the magazines *Eros, Liaison,* and the *Housewife's Handbook on Selective Promiscuity.*[30] According to the third category of the Redrup opinion, the Court should permit the punishment of those who make a profession of peddling smut and, at the same time, protect those who sell dirty books but whose minds are pure. However, since this places the judges in the position of having to make extremely complex moral and literary judgments, they have virtually ignored it.

The futility of a test which makes use of such phrases as "average person," "contemporary community standards," "dominant theme," "prurient interest," and "utterly without redeeming social importance" is obvious. These phrases naturally invite inquiry about the state of the libido of that character of legal fiction "the average man." What is "contemporary" and what are "community standards"? As for "prurient interest"— can thoughts be controlled by legislative or judicial ukase? Other questions intrude. Is there a relationship between obscenity and overt conduct such as rape and promiscuity? Is sexual stimulation always a social evil? Does repression make the pornography more desirable as a forbidden fruit?

If the state does have a legitimate interest in protecting the citizenry from being shocked and offended, sexually aroused or morally corrupted, perhaps the Supreme Court might propound a more direct approach than that used in the Redrup case. Perhaps it should adopt a clearly expressed test which would balance the nature and extent of the interest of the state in maintaining moral standards against the stake that society has in the preservation of free expression.

CENSORSHIP AND FREE PRESS

Under the Constitution, freedom of expression is protected by the First Amendment. However, the government may limit the expression of specific ideas if they are deemed to be beyond the protective mantle of the First Amendment or if the ideas are so pernicious or dangerous that censorship is necessary for the public safety and welfare. One of the underlying difficulties, however, is that, until the idea has been expressed, it is obviously uncertain whether or not it may be limited under the Constitution. At the same time, once the idea has been uttered or published, it cannot be taken back or recalled, and the evil or harm which it accomplishes cannot be retrieved. Therefore, the central problem of censorship is the difficult one of managing to safeguard those ideas which should be protected by the First Amendment and, at the same time, of deciding exactly which expressions may be restricted and of limiting them before they are disseminated. Thus, if censorship comes too late, it may be useless; if it is imposed too soon, it may destroy the significant and good ideas along with the pernicious. As a result of this problem, in many of the cases which have come before the Supreme Court, the justices have considered the way in which free speech was limited or restricted, rather than the underlying reason for the limitation.

In the thirties the Supreme Court reviewed a Minnesota statute which provided that a "malicious, scandalous, and defamatory newspaper, magazine or other periodical" could be prohibited from future publication as a public nuisance[31] While the states have always had the authority to stop a public nuisance, this case presented the conflict between that power and the right of free press. If Minnesota should be permitted to exercise its power in this way, it would mean that a newspaper could be stopped before it had printed a single issue—before anyone could actually know whether or not it deserved protection under the guarantee of free speech. The Supreme Court decided that Minnesota could not prevent future publications on the basis of a determination that past publications had violated the law. The rationale was that this would be equivalent to telling the author that he could never publish a book again because of obscenity in his first work.

However, this does not mean that all prior censorship is forbidden. When the Supreme Court was faced with the problem of whether a state requirement that a movie be shown to a censor before it could be exhibited was an unconstitutional restraint on free speech,[32] the Court decided that such a requirement, standing alone, was not violative of the First Amendment. However, a few years later, a statute authorizing censorship by the state was attacked on the ground that it allowed unreasonable restraint of free speech.[33] In this case a Maryland Act required that every motion picture be shown to a board of censors before it could be exhibited. The exhibitor could request a second showing if the board did not approve the picture. If after the second showing the film was still not approved, the exhibitor could go to the courts on appeal, a long, drawn-out procedure. However, in the interim, he could not exhibit the film.

The Supreme Court of the United States decided that this involved procedure was an unreasonable restraint of free expression and ruled that the statute was unconstitutional. Yet, in that case, the Court underscored the fact that reasonable restraints were not prohibited and might be permitted in some situations. Likewise, in 1968, the Court found objectionable a Dallas ordinance that sought to keep youngsters under sixteen from seeing movies deemed unsuitable by a local board of censors. Reflecting the views of an eight to one majority, Justice Marshall pointed out that the standards to be applied under the ordinance were so vague as to be unconstitutional.[34]

Analogous questions have come up with respect to the censorship of books, and the Supreme Court has tried to apply a test of procedural reasonableness. In 1957 the Court decided that a

New York statute was valid, even though it allowed the sale of books to be halted before it was determined whether or not the books were obscene.[35] Under the law in question the police were permitted to secure an injunction prohibiting the sale of a specific book simply because it was alleged to be obscene. The statute went on to provide that a hearing must be held within twenty-four hours to decide whether or not the material actually was obscene. In this case the Supreme Court ruled that prior censorship was permissible with such safeguards; yet, the Supreme Court has invalidated a Rhode Island act which authorized a commission to circulate a list of books deemed "objectionable for sale to minors."[36]

Currently, there is controversy over the extent to which the press should be able to report what takes place during a trial. The American Newspaper Publishers Association contends that the press must remain free, without restraint, to secure the "people's right to know." The American Bar Association, on the other hand, urges a system of restrictions, similar to Britain's, which, according to the Bar Association, safeguards a defendant's right to a fair trial. Under this system attorneys would face disciplinary proceedings or disbarment for releasing prejudicial information. In some instances, judges would be permitted to punish reporters for writing prejudicial articles during a trial.[37]

The United States Supreme Court took essentially this point of view in overthrowing the murder conviction of Sam Sheppard because of the carnival atmosphere at his trial.[38] The High Court criticized the presiding trial judge for not keeping a tighter rein on the reporters.

In the summer of 1967, Harvard Law School Professor Arthur E. Sutherland told a group of trial lawyers that he viewed the reversal of the Sheppard decision as a "crack in the armor" of what the press can and cannot print. He urged the judiciary to "step into the fray" and assert its authority over the "outside influences" which could prejudice trials.

The Supreme Court has upheld the right of the press to publish stories about both the private and public lives of individuals who become involved in public issues and events.[39] In 1964 the Court held that anyone could write defamatory items about the public life of officials and get away with it as long as malice was not established. Malice, according to the Court, was limited to the reckless disregard for the truth or the calculated lie. In that landmark case the Supreme Court held that *The New York Times* had not "recklessly disregarded truth," even though the *Times* advertising department had failed to check the accuracy of an advertisement containing news stories setting out false charges against officials of Montgomery, Alabama.

After this case, the courts threw out one libel case after another on the grounds that no malice had been established. However, there are some straws in the wind which portend a possible shift in direction. In a recent libel decision,[40] the Supreme Court made it clear that "reckless conduct is not measured by whether a reasonably prudent man would have published, or would have investigated before publishing." The Court explained, "There must be sufficient evidence to permit the conclusion that the defendant in fact entertained serious doubts as to the truth of his publication. Publishing with such doubts shows reckless disregard for truth or falsity and demonstrates actual malice." Then, Justice White opened the door to a successful libel suit a little more by making it easier to prove malice. Cries of good faith are not likely to be persuasive, said he, "when the publisher's allegations are so inherently improbable that only a reckless man would have put them in circulation." And, shortly thereafter, the court took another step in the same direction by ruling that public school teachers may not be discharged for good faith criticism of school officials, even if some of the charges turn out to be false.[41]

There has been only one case in which the Supreme Court has found actual malice to be present. It upheld a $460,000 judgment in favor of Wallace Butts, former athletic director of the

University of Georgia, who was accused in a *Saturday Evening Post* article of giving away the secrets of his football team in order to throw the game.[42] The *Post* had checked the charge of the fixed football game with a number of people, but there were many disputed quotes and questions which weakened the basis for the story. A demand not to publish the story had been turned down.

Interest has centered around an award made to former Presidential candidate Barry Goldwater, who brought a $2,000,000 libel suit against *Fact Magazine*. A special issue of that magazine reported that Senator Goldwater was afflicted with paranoia and compared him to Hitler. Among other things, it stated that he suffered "intense anxiety about his manhood" and described him as a "cruel" and practical joker. It relied on a poll of psychiatrists to substantiate its conclusions.

The verdict in Goldwater's favor apparently shows that he succeeded in convincing the jury that the accusations against him were false and that these false charges were made maliciously.[43]

5. Rights of Assembly and Petition

AMENDMENT I

THE IDEA THAT a subject may petition his ruler or government for redress of grievances is one of ancient and honorable lineage. In England this right was well established in law by 1689. The American Declaration of Independence makes it clear that the colonists, as freeborn Englishmen, had invoked this right to obtain relief, without success: "In every stage of these oppressions we have petitioned for redress in the most humble terms. Our repeated petitions have been answered only by repeated injury."

So when the American patriots formed their own government, they wanted to provide an absolute guarantee of the rights to get together with others to discuss common problems, protest those policies or acts of government considered unfair or unwise, and ask for help from the government. Thus, the right of petition, coupled with the right of assembly, was inserted into the First Amendment as a cornerstone of the Bill of Rights:

> Congress shall make no law . . . abridging . . . the right of the people peaceably to assemble and to petition the government for a redress of grievances.

The rights of assembly and petition in the Bill of Rights were guaranteed against encroachment by Congress. The law is now

74

firm in its assertion that both assembly and petition must be protected against deprivation by states or by other units of local government.[1]

These rights are not only limited to matters of citizenship. Americans are protected from governmental interference if they wish to come together or organize for any legitimate purpose, whether this be to gab, to square dance, to plan a cooperative method of selling their wheat, or to form a trade union. As a corollary, such groups may "pass the hat" and may finance bureaus of legal assistance to help their members prepare claims or fight to secure their just rights.[2]

Furthermore, indirect, sophisticated, or subtle methods of discouraging the exercise of the rights to petition or assemble would not be allowed by the Supreme Court. As an example, a local statute demanding that the National Association for the Advancement of Colored People turn over its membership lists was held to be a breach of the First Amendment. The Court felt that the situation indicated that the membership lists might be utilized to harass those who supported the organization[3]

Although through a long stretch of history the right of petition was considered more significant than the right of assembly, the right of assembly is regarded as primary today. In *DeJonge* v. *Oregon,*[4] a member of the Communist party had been convicted in the courts of Oregon for violating the Oregon Syndicalism Act. That statute defined criminal syndicalism as "the doctrine which advocates crime, physical violence, sabotage or any unlawful acts or methods as a means of accomplishing or effecting industrial or political change." The statute also made it a crime to engage in certain acts which were deemed to promote criminal syndicalism, such as "presiding at or assisting in conducting a meeting of such organization, society, or group."

DeJonge had addressed a meeting in Portland that had been convened by the Communist party. However, he had not discussed nor advocated violence or syndicalism but, rather, a current maritime strike. Following this incident, he was arrested, tried, convicted, and sentenced to serve seven years in the penitentiary.

The Supreme Court, speaking through Chief Justice Charles Evans Hughes, held that DeJonge had been deprived of his freedom of assembly and speech without due process of law. The Court pointed out that, under the construction of the statute by the lower court, it was impossible for the Communist party to meet, no matter how innocuous the subject under discussion. In its decision the Court stated, "The holding of meetings for peaceful, political action cannot be proscribed. Those who assist in the conduct of such meetings cannot be branded as criminals on that score."

The Court also indicated in this decision that, if the right of assembly was to be protected, the question must be, not who called the meeting, but what was the purpose of the meeting; not why certain people attended, "but whether their utterances transcended the bounds of freedom of speech which the Constitution protects." Thus, the Supreme Court was clearly rejecting the concept of guilt by association.

LIMITATIONS OF THESE RIGHTS

There is no guarantee in the First Amendment that anyone is secure from all restrictions on assembly and petition. The First Amendment does not promise that people may assemble for the purpose of furthering an illegal cause or of perpetrating violence. The language of the Amendment clearly and expressly speaks only of assembling "peaceably." An example is the validity of local ordinances or regulations which prohibit assembly or occupancy by more than a specified number of people because of the danger of fire. Likewise, an association can be prohibited from convening in a meeting place reserved for another association, if the purpose of the prohibition is to avoid a riot or disorder.

The test which should be applied to all these limitations is whether or not the rules or regulations are reasonable and have as their basis some legitimate public purpose. In deciding that federal employees could be prohibited from active participation in political clubs, the Supreme Court pointed out, "The essential rights of the First Amendment in some instances are subject to the elemental needs for order without which the guarantees of civil rights to others would be a mockery."[5]

Picketing and Other Union Activities

State and local governments have curtailed meetings in public places by a number of different means. The most common technique has been the requirement that a permit be obtained in advance of the meeting. These regulations have, at times, been motivated by prejudice against the purpose of the meeting, and their object has sometimes been to prevent the assembly. At other times, they have been promulgated in the honest attempt to keep traffic flowing freely and to enable the police to be present in order to give protection and to preserve public order. This dilemma has intruded itself most sharply in cases involving the trade union movement.

For the most part, the Supreme Court has stood ready to protect legitimate union activity. *Hague* v. *CIO*[6] raised the issue of the validity of a local ordinance adopted in New Jersey. This ordinance required that any group of people wishing to assemble in a public place in Jersey City must apply in advance for a permit. The municipal director of public safety was delegated the authority to refuse a permit if he felt it was necessary to do so in order to prevent riots, disturbances, or disorderly activity.

Acting under this ordinance, this director denied the CIO the right to hold meetings in Jersey City on the grounds that he felt the members were Communists and that the organization was communistic in objective. In 1939 when the dispute reached the United States Supreme Court, a majority of five to two decided that the ordinance was invalid since it permitted the director of public safety to turn down applications for public meetings simply on the basis of his opinion.

A few years later, in *Bridges* v. *California*,[7] the Supreme Court decided that a telegram sent to the California secretary of labor strongly criticizing certain actions by the state supreme court was protected under the Fourteenth Amendment as part of the right to petition.

In 1945 a state statute which made it obligatory for union leaders to register before they could sign up union members was ruled a violation of the right to peaceful assembly.[8]

In the famous case of *Thornhill* v. *Alabama*,[9] the Supreme Court confidently asserted that a law which prohibited all pick-eting, whether peaceful or not, was invalid. However, since that time, a number of cases have indicated that the rights of free speech and assembly, as expressed through picketing, are far from unlimited in America. The Supreme Court has recognized a "broad field in which a State, in enforcing some public policy, whether of its criminal, or its civil law, and whether announced by its legislature or its courts, could constitutionally enjoin peaceful picketing aimed at preventing effectuation of that policy."[10] The Supreme Court has gone so far as to hold that peaceful picketing may be restrained if, in the past, disputes between the labor and the management of a particular company have been occasions for violence.[11] This limitation has also been extended to include industries other than those actually involved in the dispute.[12]

The Court continues to recognize that picketing is basically designed to inform the public of what the dispute is all about and, hence, is entitled to the protection of the First Amendment. At the same time, picketing may serve as a powerful tool of economic coercion. Therefore, the dilemma presented by cases involving picketing in labor disputes is that of deciding where to draw the line between the right of labor to advise the public of the merits of its position and the considerably restricted right of an organized association of workers to band together in order to exert economic pressure.

Pressure Groups and Lobbies

Certainly, an important exercise of the right to petition is the activity of pressure groups and lobbyists. Since the early days of the Republic there has been persistent demand for the control of these activities. Yet, the Federalist Papers themselves attest to the valuable role played by special interest groups in a representative government. From the beginning of this century the states have been passing laws to deal with the more flagrant abuses of lobbying. Congress has conducted four investigations of the methods and purposes of professional lobbyists, and, in 1946, Congress enacted the Federal Regulation of Lobbying Act, which required the registration of lobbyists and regular reports of their contributions and expenditures.

As construed by the Supreme Court, this Act does not breach the guarantees of free speech and assembly provided for in the First Amendment. The Lobbying Act was peripherally involved in a case decided in 1953.[13] Speaking for the Court, Justice Felix Frankfurter said, that "as a matter of English," lobbying does not mean trying to influence the ideas of the community; it means, rather, presenting arguments directly "to Congress, its members or its committees." A year later the Supreme Court expressly upheld the validity of the Federal Regulation of Lobbying Act. Chief Justice Earl Warren emphasized that lobbying under the Act meant "direct communication with members of Congress on pending or proposed federal legislation"— not attempts to influence members of Congress by changing the climate of constituent opinion.[14]

INTERNAL SECURITY

With the onset of the cold war in the 1940's the interest of the Supreme Court in civil liberties seemed to diminish, except so far as these liberties involved the rights of Negroes or the threat to freedom posed by certain procedural practices. In 1956 and 1957 the Warren Court took action, with respect to the prosecution of communists and the limitation of legislative inquiries. Nevertheless, the Supreme Court has not always been consistent in the internal security cases which have arisen in the last decade or so. A certain amount of vacillation has mirrored the changes in Court personnel and the shifting of public opinion. It is diffcult under these circumstances to do more than point out some of the significant rulings of recent years.

Security and Loyalty

The Supreme Court restricted the Loyalty Review Board's efforts to start cases on its own initiative and forbid the listing of subversive groups by the Attorney-General without a hearing. Moreover, the Court decided that the aggrieved person is entitled to damages if he is fired under the security program, in the absence of a valid authorization, without an opportunity to face and cross-examine the adverse witnesses.

Yet, the Supreme Court refused to review a lower court decision that a defense contractor's employee, accused of security violation in a company report to the government, could not sue his former employer for libel.[15]

In December, 1967,[16] the Court declared that a provision of the Subversive Activities Control Act of 1950 making it a crime for Communist party members to work in a defense plant was unconstitutional unless it could be specifically shown that the defendant was an active member and that his job was a sensitive one. Shortly thereafter,[17] the Court struck down a government program aimed at keeping subversives out of the merchant marine. In the earlier case the Court threw out the law, while in the later case it held that the law did not authorize the program.

State employees seem to be protected against arbitrary state investigations. There must be some very significant public stake in the inquiry before the investigation is considered proper. A government worker cannot be fired for asserting the privilege against self-incrimination or for refusing to waive this privilege. The court prohibited what it deemed guilt by association stemming from state laws making membership in a subversive organization a conclusive proof of disloyalty. Loyalty oaths which pose a threat of dismissal to state employees must be clear in meaning. Times change, sometimes very rapidly. In 1952 the Court upheld the validity of New York's Feinberg Law, which barred subversives from employment in the public school system. Fifteen years later the Court reversed itself, ruling by a vote of five to four that the same law was unconstitutional.[18] However, states may still require teachers to sign pledges of support to the state and federal constitutions.

Rights of Aliens and Naturalized Citizens

Congress has enjoyed virtually unlimited power to control the admission of aliens into this country. Similarly, the executive branch has had almost complete authority to conduct foreign relations. As a result, for a long time the courts were careful not to become enmeshed in problems concerning the status of aliens and naturalized citizens. Gradually, however, the rights of such persons have been forfeited by more and more Court decisions.

An important example of such a case is *Rowaldt* v. *Perfetto*,[19] in which it was decided that an alien cannot be deported for membership in the Communist party, unless there is substantial evidence to prove that he was aware of the party's nature and purpose before he joined. It is a violation of the Constitution for Congress to pass a law allowing the deportation of a denaturalized citizen because he committed a crime involving moral turpitude while he was still a citizen. It is also illegal for Congress to pass a law which takes away the citizenship of a person because he returned to his land of national origin and remained there for several years or that of a native-born citizen who remained away from the United States during war time or national emergency to avoid military service. Furthermore, Congress has refused to authorize immigration officials to subpoena a naturalized citizen to testify in a hearing which is looking into his naturalization.

Legislative Investigations

About a decade ago the case of *Watkins* v. *United States*,[20] re-emphasized certain important limitations of legislative inquiry, including the principle that the legislative committee must clearly set forth the reason for and purpose of the inquiry. The purpose must be stated in the resolution authorizing the investigation, and inquiry is legitimate only if it will further some bona fide legislative objective. Witnesses cannot be subjected to fishing expeditions into their personal affairs simply for the purpose of exposing these affairs to the public limelight. Witnesses are also protected against self-incrimination and unreasonable search and seizure.

Perhaps most significant is the fact that legislative inquiries, whether federal or state, cannot ask answers which would violate the rights of the witness to free speech and association, except when the threat to public safety is so great that it outweighs the guarantees of freedom of expression.

The Right to Travel

In 1964 the Supreme Court invalidated the passport section of the Subversive Activities Control Act. The Court decided that the portion of this statute which prevented members of communist-controlled groups from obtaining passports violated the Constitution since it too broadly and indiscriminately "restricts the right to travel."[21]

THE RIGHT TO DEMONSTRATE

Every day the newspapers recite the details of some sort of demonstration. These demonstrations have taken many exotic forms and have had widely varying objectives. There have been sit-ins, teach-ins, lie-ins, sleep-ins, and even swim-ins. These demonstrations have not only related to labor disputes, but have also concerned civil rights, the draft, South Vietnam, disarmament, apartheid, school administration, and demands for hot lunches for children. The increasing use of this technique has pointed up the need for clarification of how far the organized community, i.e., the state or municipality, can go in order to maintain public order without unduly encroaching on freedom of expression.

Demonstrations present certain problems over and above those involved in free speech. There is the additional factor of overt conduct, which may certainly be more conducive to violence or public disorder than speech, alone.

The Supreme Court has recognized this difference. In *Cox* v. *Louisiana*,[22] the Court said:

> We emphatically reject the notion urged by appellant that the First and Fourteenth Amendments afford the same kind of freedom to those who would communicate ideas by conduct such as patrolling, marching and picketing on streets and high-

ways, as these amendments afford to those who communicate ideas by pure speech.

Police officials, because of their work, sometimes feel that the free expression of ideas by demonstrations often brings in its wake violence, intimidation, and, as a matter of fact, interference with free speech.

The director of the Third Division of the New York City Police Department, which covers most of mid-Manhattan, puts it this way:

> Any time you have a crowd, you have to be prepared for certain eventualities—obstruction of movement, panic, violence, etc.
> . . . Crowds are much easier to handle when mobile. An obstruction is always a source of trouble because it, more than unpopular speech or demonstrations for unpopular causes, can lead to short tempers and violence.
> . . . Many civilians will come up to the police and demand to know why certain people are arrested. In some neighborhoods, people may be more resentful than in others. . . . Some people are resentful of non-conformist dress and appearance.
> . . . In general we plan ahead to police the viewers as well as the demonstrators, making use of whatever information we may have about each.[23]

The various types of disorder which have been considered sufficient to justify restriction of the right to demonstrate include violence, obstruction of traffic, intimidation of courts, picketing for an unlawful purpose, and extreme noise.[24]

The law is clear that the demonstration loses its protection under the Constitution when it is the cause of substantial disorder. However, even when there is no actual disorder, the protection may be lost because of the existence of a "clear and present danger" of a breach of the peace.

There is only one case,[25] in which the Supreme Court applied the "clear and present danger" test to sustain a conviction resulting from a demonstration where there had been no actual violence. In that case, about seventy-five or eighty people, both

Negro and white, had gotten together on a street corner in Syracuse, New York. The defendant, a man named Feiner, had apparently been urging Negroes to rise up in arms and fight for equal rights. These words of "incitement to riot" caused the restless gathering to become more excited and to press about Feiner. One person in the crowd threatened violence if the two policemen who were there "did not act." Feiner refused to desist, although there were three police requests that he do so. He was arrested and later convicted of disorderly conduct. The Supreme Court affirmed the conviction and applied the test of "clear and present danger" concluding:

> The findings of the New York courts as to the condition of the crowd and the refusal of the petitioner to obey the police requests . . . are persuasive that the conviction of the petitioner for violation of public peace, order and authority does not exceed the balance of proper state police action.

In a number of recent demonstration cases the Court has seemed quite reluctant to find the existence of a clear and present danger. *Edwards* v. *South Carolina*[26] concerned the convictions of about one hundred ninety demonstrators who marched on to the state house grounds at Columbia, South Carolina for the purpose of protesting racial segregation. There were thirty or more police officers present and about three hundred spectators, including some "possible troublemakers." There were no hostile remarks, no obstruction of traffic, no actual violence or threat of violence by the demonstrators. The demonstrators clapped their hands, stamped their feet, sang songs and listened to a "religious harangue" by one of their leaders. When the demonstrators refused to obey the order of the city manager to march on and disperse, they were arrested. The Supreme Court reversed the convictions.

In a later case, *Cox* v. *Louisiana*,[27] about two thousand people got together in front of the state courthouse where several demonstrators who had been arrested the day before were in jail. The demonstrators were 5 feet deep, but they did not obstruct the street, even though they occupied almost the entire block. They waved signs and sang songs, which brought about a response from their colleagues in the courthouse jail. Cox spoke to the group and concluded with a plea to "sit-in" at uptown lunch counters. The sheriff construed this as being inflammatory and ordered the group to disperse. They refused, and the sheriff finally resorted to the use of tear gas. Cox was arrested the next day and was convicted of disturbing the peace, obstructing public pastures, and courthouse picketing. The Supreme Court again set aside these convictions and described the case as "a far cry from the situation in *Feiner* v. *New York.*"

A comparison of the Feiner case with the cases of Edwards and Cox seems to make it plain that a "clear and present danger" of disorder will be found only in those instances where there is a combination of inadequate police protection, words of incitement from demonstrators, threats of disorder from spectators and obstruction of free passage. The omission of one or more of these elements, may mean that the situation cannot be considered to constitute a "clear and present danger."

There are three available methods by which the State can maintain orderly demonstrations. The first is to punish unlawful acts by the demonstrators through use of the various provisions of the criminal law. Another is to have a licensing ordinance which requires a permit in advance of the demonstration. The third is to apply to the courts in an appropriate situation for an injunction regulating the conduct of the demonstrators. The line between insurrection and legitimate expression is a nettlesome one. This can be seen in the case of William Epton[28] who shrieked "We will not be fully free until we smash the state completely and totally," to the crowd gathered on the first evening of the riots which took place in the streets of Harlem in 1964. Shortly later that same night Epton advised, "In that process, we're going to have to kill a lot of these cops, a lot of these judges, and we'll have to go up against their army." Epton, who had left the Communist party because he felt it restricted him too much in advancing his ideas, was convicted by the court in New York of conspiring to riot and advancing and conspiring to advocate criminal anarchy. He appealed his conviction and his one year concurrent sentence to the Supreme Court of the United States.[28]

It was anticipated that the High Court would use this case as a pulpit from which to tell how far demonstrators and their leaders can go before the First Amendment guarantee of free speech yields to the necessity of protecting the public from riots and rampage. However, the Court ignored this chance and dismissed Epton's appeal with an unsigned order. As more and more groups resort to demonstrations to forcefully indicate their views and to influence the government and private groups, the dilemma of balancing the public interests in both keeping order and preserving free speech becomes more difficult and more painful.

ANTI-WAR ACTION AS SYMBOLIC SPEECH

In the name of the "Poor People's Campaign," an indignant band of youngsters blew off steam by hurling rocks through the windows of the Supreme Court. Was this act a crime or was it "symbolic speech" protected by the First Amendment?

The Supreme Court has cast the protective mantle of free speech over such acts as the flying of a red banner, the carrying of placards by union pickets, the salute to the American flag, and sit-ins in a public library. However, Chief Justice Warren sought to limit the extent to which action can be regarded as symbolic speech. He once wrote, "We cannot accept the view that an apparently limitless variety of conduct can be labeled 'speech' whenever the person engaging in the conduct intends thereby to express an idea."

The case[29] in which this view was expressed began on a chilly day in March, 1966, when four youths ignited their draft cards with a cigarette lighter on the steps of the South Boston Court-house. These acts had been well advertised in advance, so well, in fact, that the boys were apprehended by FBI agents. The youths were arrested and convicted, for not carrying their draft card as required by the Liberty Service Act of 1948. One of the young men, David P. O'Brien, appealed his conviction. How-ever, in a seven to one decision, the Supreme Court upheld the Congressional Act by comparing the burning of draft cards to the destruction of tax records.

Justice Warren, groping to find a more precise definition of symbolic speech, wrote that acts of dissent can be punished if the government has "an important or substantial and constitu-tional interest in forbidding them, if the incidental restriction on expression is no greater than necessary, and if the government's real interest is not to squelch dissent."

An even more basic conflict in democratic values underlies this controversy. Erwin Griswald, former Dean of the Harvard Law School and now U.S. Solicitor General, put it this way in a speech at Tulane University Law School:

> One who contemplates civil disobedience should not be sur-prised and must not be bitter if a criminal conviction ensues. It is part of the Gandhian tradition that the sincerity of the in-dividual's conscience presupposes that the law will punish this assertion of personal principle.

He summed it up by saying, "It is the essence of law that it binds all alike, irrespective of personal motive." This is true whether the protestor decides "to halt a troop train to protect the Viet Nam war" or whether he "fires shots into a civil rights leader's home to protest integration."

These sentiments were echoed by Earl Morris, President of the American Bar Association, speaking at Syracuse Law School. He stated, "Many today seem to be demanding for themselves the unlimited right to disobey the law. . . . An essen-tial concomitant of civil disobedience is the actor's willingness to accept the punishment that follows."

6. Security of Person and Home

AMENDMENTS II, III and IV

FREEDOM TO THINK one's thoughts without interference and to disseminate one's ideas is protected from government interference under the First Amendment. There are two other freedoms which are of almost equal importance. They are the security of one's physical being and the sanctity of one's abode. The Second, Third, and Fourth Amendments were designed to throw a network of protection over these freedoms.

THE RIGHT TO BEAR ARMS

Reliance on self-help is a major theme in the history and psychology of America. All thrill to the story of the Minutemen, those doughty denizens of the colonies, who, upon a moment's notice, gathered to protect their little homes, their flowering fields, and their loved ones. The revolutionists of 1776 regarded a large standing army with misgivings and suspicion. It was not surprising, therefore, that the delegates to the Constitutional Convention shared the feeling of Elbridge Gerry that such a national military establishment was the "bane of liberties."

Apparently, they felt that, in times of national peril, an army could be garnered from the reservoir of citizens organized into local militias. As incorporated into the Bill of Rights, the Second Amendment, which was drafted to reflect this viewpoint, provided:

> A well regulated militia, being necessary to the security of a free state, the right of the people to keep and bear arms, shall not be infringed.

Because this amendment was designed to protect the local and state militias from interference by the national government, the Court has decided that it does not apply to the states,[1] and, since the federal government has never gone very far in an attempt to take over the local militias, there are no cases which throw light on this aspect of the Second Amendment. However, the express language used in this constitutional provision makes it fair to assume that the militias are secure from encroachment by the federal government.

While the Second Amendment is directed to the preservation of local militias, it does not serve to assure any citizen that he may own or use firearms.[2] The ownership and use of a gun is subject to reasonable regulation by the federal government, as well as by localities. The pleas of those citizens who argue that they are entitled to keep guns in order to protect themselves or to be ready to help their country are not supported by the cases interpreting the Constitution. The Second Amendment does not preclude the federal government from reasonably restricting the manufacture or shipment in interstate commerce of firearms, nor does it bar the government from taxing such transactions.[3]

In a like manner, the states may pass laws which govern the ownership and use of firearms, providing that such regulation is reasonable. Many states and other localities have statutes or ordinances which impose licensing requirements on the possession of guns, prohibit certain categories of persons from owning firearms, or forbid the use of such weapons during certain times and in certain places.

SECURITY OF THE HOME

The Third Amendment is today a museum piece, reflecting the history of the United States. It does not seem to serve any practical purpose at the present time.

Before the American Revolution, the British king maintained military troops in the colonies. These soldiers were, at times, housed in private homes, rather than in military barracks. The colonials were quite bitter about this threat to their tranquility, their privacy, and their womenfolk. Thus, it is not surprising to find that, in the Declaration of Independence, the Americans inveighed against the British Crown, "for quartering large bodies of armed troops among us."

It was unquestionably the memories of this practice which prompted the draftsmen of the Bill of Rights to propose the Third Amendment:

> No soldier shall, in time of peace be quartered in any house without the consent of the owner, nor in time of war, but in a manner to be prescribed by law.

The Third Amendment certainly applies to the federal government. Although there have been no cases raising the question, it seems safe to say that this amendment does not bind the states. The meaning of the Third Amendment seems fairly clear: A property owner cannot be required to house federal soldiers in times of peace. While he may be compelled to lodge troops in wartime, it may only be pursuant to a general law describing the procedures to be followed.

In 1951 the validity of a rent control act was challenged. Among other things, the petition claimed that the law was unconstitutional because "the Housing and Rent Act, as amended and extended, is and always was the incubator hatchery of swarms of bureaucrats to be quartered as storm troopers upon the people in violation of Amendment III of the United States Constitution."[4] The court gave short shrift to this contention.

RESTRICTIONS ON SEARCH AND SEIZURE

The framers of the Bill of Rights knew full well the terror of a "midnight knock at the door" and of arbitrary arrest. They knew the evil of the invasion of an individual's household for abusive search and seizure. It was the determination that this should not happen here which created compelling impetus for the adoption of the Fourth Amendment.

By the time of the American Revolution these rights had become recognized in England through many bitter controversies. Yet, the British did not concede that the colonists had similar rights. This refusal to acknowledge that the settlers were entitled to the rights of freeborn Englishmen was a significant source of irritation leading to the American Revolution. What was most infuriating to the American colonists were the Writs of Assistance, which gave local English officials almost unrestricted authority to enter and search the homes of private citizens and to seize their belongings.

The patriot James Otis in 1761, condemned these writs as "the worst instruments of arbitrary power," inasmuch as they surrendered "the liberty of every man in the hands of every petty officer."[5] This stake in personal privacy, the interest in security from arbitrary arrest or unreasonable intrusion into one's home, was uppermost in the minds of the Revolutionists. Because of such strong feelings, many of the state constitutions incorporated very specific guarantees against arbitrary action by tyrannical officials. A good example is the broad provision inserted into the Massachusetts Constitution of 1780. This provision served as a model for the federal clause,[6] and, thus, the Fourth Amendment emerged in the following language:

> The right of the people to be secure in their persons, houses, papers, and effects, against unreasonable searches and seizures, shall not be violated, and no warrants shall issue, but upon probable cause, supported by oath or affirmation, and particu-

larly describing the place to be searched, and the persons or things to be seized.

While, as originally drafted, the Fourth Amendment applied only to federal office holders, it is now clear that the same restriction has been absorbed into the Fourteenth Amendment and, thus, also limits what local officials can do.[7]

Protection Against Unlawful Arrest

One usually thinks of the Fourth Amendment as a bulwark against illegal search and seizure of personal property. Yet, it is just as important as a bar to the improper seizure of individuals —that is, to invalid arrests. It is not always necessary to actually restrain a person by force, or even to make a formal statement to him, in order to have effected an arrest in the contemplation of the law. However, an arrest must involve more than just stopping a person in order to ask him some questions in the process of a routine investigation. The arrest takes place when an individual is considered to be detained by the policemen:

> . . . For there to be an arrest, it is not necessary that there be an application of physical force, or manual touching of the body, or physical restraint which may be visible to the eye or a formal declaration of arrest. It is sufficient if the person arrested understands that he is in the power of the one arresting, and submits in consequence.[8]

Arrest Without a Warrant

It is entirely possible for a policeman to effect a lawful arrest without first obtaining a warrant. While it is true that the Fourth Amendment prohibits an arrest where there is no basis for it in law, the amendment does not impose the requirement that the policeman must always obtain a warrant as a prerequisite for an arrest. Generally, there are two situations in which a law enforcement officer may make an arrest without a warrant: When the policeman who makes the arrest actually sees a misdemeanor or felony, such as a trespass, an assault, or an armed robbery, being committed; and when the policeman who makes the arrest has "probable cause" to believe that a felony, rather than a misdemeanor, has been committed, that the person he is arresting has committed it, and that the facts and circumstances of the situation justify an arrest without taking the time to obtain a warrant.

Most of the disputes concerning arrests without a warrant have revolved around the question of whether or not there was "probable cause" to believe that a felony had been committed. The courts have discovered that it is much easier to propound a rule covering the validity of arrests without a warrant than to apply such formula to a specific set of facts in a case to be decided.

In one case,[9] federal narcotics agents received a tip from an informer who, in the past, had shown himself to be accurate and reliable. He advised them that a person named Draper was peddling narcotics in Denver. He also informed them that Draper was leaving for Chicago to obtain a supply of narcotics and would return to Denver by train on a certain day. He described Draper as a man who walked fast and who would be carrying a tan zipper bag. On the day in question, a man corresponding to Draper's description got off the train arriving from Chicago. The agents arrested him and the Supreme Court decided that, under the circumstances, there had been the "probable cause" so that a warrant was not required.

Compare this decision with the facts and result of another case decided by the Supreme Court.[10] In this case the arrest was made on the basis of information given by a person who had himself been arrested. Relying on this tip, narcotics agents arrested a man at his home. The High Court held that there was no "probable cause" to justify the arrest in the absence of a warrant since the informant was not shown to have been a reliable and regular purveyor of information, although he was known to the authorities.

On the basis of even these few cases, it is apparent that it is impossible to formulate an entirely satisfactory test of what constitutes "probable cause." Perhaps as accurate or, at least, as helpful a statement on this subject as can be found in the law books was expressed over a century ago when the Supreme Court stated that "probable cause" must consist of such facts and circumstances as would "excite the belief" in the mind of a reasonable man that the suspect was guilty of the crime in question.[11]

Arrest With a Warrant

When an arrest is made under a warrant obtained in advance, the warrant must meet the requirements set out in the Fourth Amendment. As has been explained, it must be grounded on "probable cause." The alleged crime which forms the basis for the issuance of the warrant must be described in an affidavit sworn to or affirmed by the policeman or other person seeking the warrant. In addition the warrant must be very specific in its description of the person to be arrested. A law enforcement official cannot secure a blank warrant to be filled in at his convenience. If the warrant does not meet these requirements, it is invalid. If it is invalid, then the arrest itself is unlawful.

Habeas Corpus and Other Remedies

To the person who is being detained, it matters little, at the moment, whether he has been arrested lawfully or unlawfully. So far as he is concerned, the important thing is to regain his freedom. The Fourth Amendment standing alone would be illusory without some way of giving force to its requirements. Fortunately, the Constitution itself furnishes one effective tool for making the guarantees of the Fourth Amendment work.

Article I of the Constitution contains express authority for the venerable writ of habeas corpus. This writ has been the time-tested means for securing relief from unlawful detention. The person who has been illegally arrested can obtain, from the appropriate court, a writ of habeas corpus requiring the police to release him.

Habeas corpus has provided the golden key to the freedom persisting throughout the legal history of America and, in fact, to its English antecedents. Article I, Section 9, Clause 2 of the original Constitution provides:

> The privilege of the writ of habeas corpus shall not be suspended, unless when in cases of rebellion or invasion the public safety may require it.

Habeas corpus stands, therefore, as a remedy for any unlawful detention, not simply one resulting from an arrest. The writ can be invoked to secure the release of a person improperly held in a mental hospital, in the military forces, or by the immigration authorities. It can even be used to free a person from a wrongful private confinement, as in the case of a student improperly retained in a boarding school.

In the spring of 1968 the Supreme Court held that, although federal law permits only persons who are "in custody" to challenge, by habeas corpus proceedings, the legality of their detention, a prisoner is "in custody" when he is serving a prior sentence, and, thus, in this case should not be required to delay in seeking court assistance.[12] The Court also overruled its prior view that the appeal of a habeas corpus case becomes moot when the prisoner completes his term and is released. This new decision came about in connection with the case of James P. Carafas,[13] who was convicted of burglary and larceny in 1960 and was paroled in 1964. The Court ruled that, even though he had served his jail sentence, he still suffered disabilities as a convicted felon and should be permitted to complete his appellate challenge to his convictions.

What are the mechanics for procuring a writ of habeas

corpus? The person who is trying to get the writ initiates a civil proceeding against the prison warden, or whoever has actual custody of the person being retained. When the court receives the petition, it will order that the prisoner be brought before it, unless the judge feels he can decide the validity of the detention on the basis of what appears on the petition and on the papers accompanying it. After argument and, if necessary, the production of the prisoner, the prisoner will be ordered released if he is being held improperly.

There are other possible remedies for unlawful arrest, such as penal code provisions directed against policemen who act improperly and civil suits for money damages. But the most direct method is still the traditional petition for habeas corpus.

Search and Seizure of Property

The Fourth Amendment guarantees that "persons, houses, papers, and effects," shall be secure from "unreasonable searches and seizures." Obviously, all searches and seizures are not prohibited, nor is there a requirement that a warrant must be obtained in every case before the search and seizure. But, if there is to be a search and seizure without a warrant, the amendment does require that these acts be justified on reasonable grounds.

In the wake of the murder of a Baltimore policeman by two men described as Negroes, the police, acting only on unsubstantiated "tips," searched three hundred homes in the Negro section of the city without warrants. In the summer of 1967 hordes of armed national guardsmen and state troopers moved in to reinforce municipal policemen in a house to house search of a Negro neighborhood in Plainfield, New Jersey. The city, on the outskirts of the area in which the Newark riots were taking place, was declared to be in a "state of disaster and emergency" by the governor. It had been learned that forty-six rifles were missing from a nearby firearms plant.[14]

These two incidents point up the need to evaluate the balance between the authority of government officials to act in emergencies and the constitutional limits on the power of such officials.

Search and Seizure With a Warrant

When search and seizure is based upon a warrant, the warrant must satisfy the requirements set forth in the Fourth Amendment, as well as any additional requirements called for by the laws of the particular state involved.

Usually, if a police officer wishes to search a person's home or possessions, he must obtain a warrant before he acts. This warrant is a legal document issued by a judge. The warrant must be based on facts stated under oath or an affirmation of the official asking for the warrant. "It must be quite specific in the way it describes the place to be searched, and the persons or things to be seized." In the classic phrase, the warrant cannot authorize a "fishing expedition."

Under the Fourth Amendment, these are standards which federal law enforcement agents must obey; and, under the Fourteenth Amendment, state and local policemen must comply with them as well. These restrictions insure "the right of the people to be secure in their persons, houses, papers, and effects against unreasonable searches and seizures" and guarantee that "No warrants shall issue but upon probable cause, supported by oath or affirmation. . . ."

Even though an officer may believe most sincerely that someone has committed a crime, this is not enough to justify the issuance of a search warrant. The application of the warrant must be supported by facts showing reasonable grounds for the belief. Before the judge issues the warrant, he will satisfy himself that there is "probable cause" for its need.

Search and Seizure Without a Warrant

Under some circumstances a search and seizure, even without a warrant, is justified under law; but these circumstances are limited. In each case of this sort the court will review what happened to decide whether the particular search was justified and reasonable. There are some situations in which the law permits exception to the requirement of a warrant.

It is permissible to make a search and seizure, even without a search warrant, when the person involved has unequivocally and clearly given his consent. However, this consent must be given voluntarily and knowingly. If the person does not know that he has a right to refuse to allow the projected search, or if he is frightened by the police, this vitiates the ostensible consent. As the Supreme Court said in one case:

> Entry to defendant's living room, which was the beginning of the search, was demanded on the color of office. It was granted in submission to authority rather than as an understanding and intentionable waiver of a constitutional right.[15]

A second condition under which no warrant is required for search and seizure occurs when a person's business, occupation, or profession requires him to maintain certain records which are available for public inspection. These are considered "public records" and are not within the protection afforded by the Fourth Amendment.[16]

The officials who are interested in these records do not need a warrant to examine or seize them. Even in this situation, however, the investigation of the records must be done at a reasonable hour of a reasonable day, and the examination itself must be reasonable. Public officials cannot barge into a private home or office or place of business at any hour of the night and rummage indiscriminately through all the papers lying around. This would constitute an illegal "fishing expedition," no matter whether the records are public or private. For example, a physician who is required by law to keep a record of the narcotics he has on hand cannot refuse to let the proper agents examine those records, provided that the investigation is conducted at a reasonable time and that the examination itself is reasonable.

In a few situations, the courts have permitted search and seizure without a warrant and even without consent of the person subjected to the action of the police. It has been recognized, for instance, that some latitude must be allowed to policemen who feel that a certain automobile should be searched. The underlying reason for this latitude is that autos can be moved quickly from one place to another, making it almost impossible to obtain a search warrant in time. In one case[17] revenue agents were conducting undercover operations. They made arrangements with the suspect to purchase illegal liquor and jotted down the description of the car and its license number. Several months later, they spotted the automobile and noticed that it seemed heavily laden. They stopped the car and searched it without a warrant. The officers discovered sixty-eight bottles of liquor. The Supreme Court ruled that the search and seizure was permissible and emphasized that there is a considerable difference between allowing the search of a stationary structure, such as a dwelling, and that of an automobile, which can be moved quickly.

A court may uphold the search of a person who was properly arrested, even though a search warrant had not been obtained in advance. The place where the arrest was made or the suspect was apprehended may sometimes be searched as well, depending on the circumstances.[18] An interesting example of such a "contemporaneous search" is the case of a rare stamp dealer who sold some false items to a collector. The police obtained a warrant for his arrest and then proceeded to arrest him at his place of business. After going through his desk, safe, file cabinets, and the rest of his one room office, they seized the 573 stamps they found there. The Supreme Court was faced with the question of whether or not the search and seizure was violative of the Constitution. The majority upheld the action on the grounds that the one small room searched was the scene of the illegal activity, that it was under the direct and complete control of the accused, and that it was open to the public for this business.[19]

In 1962 two private citizens pursued an armed thief into a house which they had followed him to after a robbery. They then called the police. When the officers arrived, Mrs. Bennie Joe Hayden permitted them to enter. They found Mr. Hayden in bed without any clothes on, and, later, they discovered his garments and two guns in the washing machine. Hayden's ultimate conviction was based upon the identification of his clothing by several eyewitnesses to the crime.

Under the rule which existed before the Hayden case, only four kinds of evidence could be seized by the police. These were the proceeds of a crime; the tools with which the crime was committed; the objects that made an escape possible; and items that are illegal because of their essential nature, such as narcotics. Nothing else could be seized, since no other object could be used as evidence.

In the Hayden case the Supreme Court went beyond this old rule and held that the yield of a reasonable search may be used as legal evidence to convict an accused even though the objects do not fall into one of the four previously accepted categories.[20]

It is impossible to detail in advance all those situations in which a search and seizure without a warrant are permissible. The basic principle is that, when no consent has been given, the individuals and their private belongings cannot be searched or seized without a warrant, unless this is justified by the circumstances of the particular case and the police acts are carried out in a reasonable manner.

Electronic Search and Seizure

As a result of modern technology it is possible to intrude on the conversation of an individual, either by tapping his telephone wires or through use of other electronic devices. It seems clear, at the present time, that the Constitution restricts but does not prohibit such invasion of privacy. In a case decided by the High Court in December of 1967, it was held that eavesdropping is permissible within certain limits.[21] In this case Justice Potter Stewart, speaking for the majority, wrote that it makes no difference whether the bugging is accomplished in a public place or in a home. He pointed out that the Fourth Amendment was designed to "protect people, not places." Nor does there have to be an actual entry or trespass into a place before the Fourth Amendment is violated. Since modern electronic devices do not require actual physical attachment or trespass, Justice Stewart noted that the protection of the Constitution "cannot turn on the presence or absence of a physical intrusion."

The situation before the Court in this case involved a petty Los Angeles gambler, who had made incriminating calls from a public telephone booth. The FBI had bugged the telephone with a device which had been taped onto the outside of the booth. The officers had not obtained a warrant in advance. It was conceded both that the agents had not used the bugging device until they had had a good reason to believe that the suspect was employing the telephone to violate the federal law and that they had been careful to stop listening as soon as they had heard the conversations related to the case at hand.

Justice Stewart explained:

> This surveillance was so narrowly circumscribed that a duly authorized magistrate, properly notified of the need for such investigation, specifically informed of the basis on which it was to proceed and clearly apprised of the precise intrusion it would

entail, could constitutionally have authorized the very limited search and seizure that the Government asserts took place.

The reason that the conviction of the defendant, Charles Katz, was set aside was the failure of the agents to obtain a warrant.

As a result of this seven to one decision, it seems permissible for the police to use any one of many new electronic devices in order to eavesdrop, provided that a warrant for its use is obtained in advance. Under the doctrine of the Katz case it is possible to eavesdrop without violating the Constitution if the policeman first goes before the appropriate judge and secures a warrant by showing probable cause. The officers must conduct the eavesdropping within the limitations set by the judge, and, after the surveillance, the officer must return to the court to reveal what was overheard.

On June 17, 1968, the Supreme Court ruled that criminal evidence obtained by police listening in on a party line conversation may not be introduced as incriminating evidence in a state trial. The majority held that, since the participants in the telephone conversations had not consented to the police's eavesdropping, tape recordings of the conversation could not be used as evidence.[22] This ruling has stimulated agitation for legislation which will permit more relaxed rules with reference to police eavesdropping.

Limits on "Stop and Frisk"

The police officer is in a bind when he does not have enough evidence to make an arrest, yet to his experienced eye, a character going down the street seems to be behaving in a suspicious way. Law enforcement officials argue that, if they are to have any real control over rising crime in the streets, they must have the authority to stop, detain, question, and search suspects.

The controversy centers around that part of the Fourth Amendment which says that the "right of the people to be secure in their persons against unreasonable searches and seizures shall not be violated, and no warrants shall issue, but upon probable cause." Opponents of the "stop and frisk" laws have interpreted this to mean that no person can be held by force or searched unless the law enforcement agents have probable cause to believe that a crime has been committed and that the suspect has committed it. Those speaking for the police have contended that, historically, policemen have been permitted to detain and question persons who seem suspicious and that the Fourth Amendment does not prohibit this as long as the action by the officer is not unreasonable. The critical word is "unreasonable."

Justice Warren, speaking for an eight to one majority, has decided that a police officer may challenge a person if there is good reason to believe that that person is looking for trouble. The policeman may also search for arms if there is reason to think that the suspect is carrying a weapon.[23]

The policeman cannot rely on mere speculation or "inarticulate hunches." What counts is "whether a reasonably prudent man in the circumstances would be warranted in the belief that his safety or that of others was in danger." The "police officer must be able to point to specific . . . facts" which motivated him to take action.

The objective of the frisk can only be to find a hidden weapon. However, if a frisk is justified and it discloses other incriminating evidence, such evidence may be introduced in court. The Supreme Court has conceded that this test is not as precise as it might be; but it does represent an attempt to establish a test less rigorous than the "probable cause" required to validate an arrest. The way that the court may be expected to apply this test of the "reasonably prudent" policeman is illustrated by the following three cases decided by the Court.

In one case[24] a detective noticed two men pacing back and forth and peering into a Cleveland store window. They seemed to be "casing" the establishment in preparation for a robbery, so the officer halted and frisked them. They were both found to be carrying arms and were convicted on that ground. The Court upheld the convictions on the theory that the detective had acted in a reasonable manner under the circumstances.

A New York City policeman, hearing a noise in the apartment house where he lived, investigated and saw two men stealthily moving in the hallway. The policeman pulled out his service gun and went into the hall. The two bolted, and the policeman, in hot pursuit, nabbed one of them on the stairway. The ensuing frisk revealed that the apprehended man was carrying burglar's tools, a crime. The High Court was well satisfied that the frisk was reasonable and held that the resulting conviction was proper.

The decision was different in the case of a man who was known to consort with narcotics addicts.[25] A Brooklyn police officer had kept this man under surveillance for eight hours. The police officer conceded that, during that time, he had not observed anything that seemed suspicious. Yet, he had walked over to the suspect and said, "You know what I'm after." The suspect put his hand into one of his pockets. Almost instantaneously the policeman lunged for the pocket and his fingers closed around a glassine packet of heroin.

The Supreme Court reversed the man's conviction on the grounds that the mere fact that the suspect had frequently been seen in the company of known narcotics users did not give the policeman a proper basis for stopping or frisking the suspect. The majority opinion was that the circumstances were not enough to cause "a reasonable fear of life or limb. The police officer is not entitled to seize and search every person he sees on the street and of whom he makes enquiries."

Evidence Unlawfully Obtained—The Exclusionary Rule

Suppose that, as a result of evidence obtained by an illegal search and seizure, the suspect is convicted and sent to jail? How does it help the person serving time to know that the Constitution has been violated, or that he may sue the officer who seized the evidence unlawfully, or even that the officer himself has been sent to jail?

Over a long period of time the Supreme Court has decided that the most effective way to insure the enforcement of the Fourth Amendment is to make its violation the basis for throwing out evidence which comes about as a result of such illegal action. If the evidence secured by means of an illegal search and seizure cannot be used to convict, then, perhaps policemen would lose the incentive to search and seize without complying with the law. The result of this judicial analysis is the exclusionary rule. Evidence obtained by the police in violation of the Fourth Amendment or of any statute is inadmissible as evidence in court.[26]

In the leading case of *Weeks* v. *United States*[27] the Supreme Court decided that the Fourth Amendment "might as well be stricken from the Constitution," if federal law enforcement agents were permitted to use illegally seized evidence in order to convict a defendant. The Court held that the federal courts could not accept evidence obtained in direct violation of the Fourth Amendment. Any evidence obtained in that manner must be overturned in order to discourage violation of the Fourth Amendment.

However, it soon became apparent that simply forbidding the use of illegally obtained evidence was not enough to stop unlawful searches and seizures. Federal officials were still using such evidence as a lead or to encourage a suspect to confess to a crime.

In *Nardone* v. *United States*[28] the High Court labeled this indirect evidence as the "fruit of the poisonous tree." It then held that the evidence which grew out of the illegally obtained material could not be employed in the federal courts. If the tree itself was poisoned, then the fruit suffered from the same taint.

Although the federal law was changing, police officers could still generally rely on illegally obtained evidence to secure convictions in the state courts. As a consequence, there was little to discourage violation of the Constitution except the policeman's oath of office. As a matter of fact, the state police could obtain evidence illegally and cooperate with their more restricted federal colleagues by sharing it with them.

The Supreme Court resolved this incongruity in *Elkins* v. *United States*,[29] which held that federal agents could not use evidence illegally obtained and "handed to them on a silver platter" by state police. As a result of this ruling, all evidence obtained directly or indirectly through violation of the Fourth Amendment was effectively barred from the federal courts.

In the state courts, however, material obtained in violation of the Constitution continued to be admitted into evidence. The Supreme Court refused to extend the exclusionary rule of the federal courts to limit the states unless the state law also required exclusion of such evidence or unless, in a particular case, the circumstances were so unjust as to "shock the conscience of the court."[30]

Finally, with the landmark case of *Mapp* v. *Ohio*,[31] the Supreme Court laid down the rule that neither the federal nor the state courts may admit evidence which has come about as a result of an illegal search or seizure. On June 3, 1968, on the basis of this rule, the Court set aside the conviction of a North Carolina Negro sentenced to life imprisonment for raping a white girl and shooting her and her boyfriend.[32] The Court ruled that a rifle found during a search without a warrant of the house of the defendant's grandmother had been improperly admitted into evidence.

7. The Right to Life, Liberty and Property

AMENDMENT V

A DOMINANT THEME in the development of the American constitutional system has been the concept that every person is entitled to a fair hearing in legal matters which are important to him. Judge Curtis Bok of the Philadelphia Court of Common Pleas vividly expressed this idea by writing:

> In the whole history of law and order the longest step forward was taken by primitive man, when, as if by common consent, the tribe sat down in a circle and allowed only one man to speak at a time. An accused who is shouted down has no rights whatever. Unless people have an instinct for procedure their conception of basic human rights is a waste of effort, and wherever we see a negation of these rights it can be traced to a lack, an inadequacy, or a violation of procedure.

While the controversy concerning the exact meaning and application of Chapter 39 of the Magna Carta has never been completely resolved,[1] it is agreed that King John acquiesced to the demands of the barons and bishops, at least to the extent of promising not to take action against them in an arbitrary manner. It was assured that there would be notice of the charge and a hearing of the complaint in accordance with the "law of the land."[2]

The abiding importance of the Magna Carta lies in the fact that so many struggles for freedom have been fought and won in the name of the principles enunciated in this great document.

THE RIGHT TO A GRAND JURY

The Magna Carta recognized that a man should not be tried for a serious crime unless a grand jury could sift the facts and decide whether they warranted further consideration at a trial. By the time the Declaration of Independence was written, the grand jury system was deeply rooted in the administration of criminal justice. However, many of the leaders at the Constitutional Convention were fearful that it might be taken away if it were not more firmly secured. They still shuddered over the implications of the case of Peter Zenger in New York. The Royal Governor there, in the attempt to intimidate Zenger, who was publishing unfriendly articles in his newspaper, tried to force the grand jury into indicting him. The grand jury felt that sufficient grounds for indictment had not been shown. To its credit, and to the everlasting benefit of a free press, the grand jury remained adamant and refused to indict.

The possibility that similar attempts might be made in the future impelled the First Congress to incorporate a specific provision into the Fifth Amendment. The Fifth Amendment to the Constitution, therefore, included the following:

> No person shall be held to answer for a capital, or otherwise infamous crime, unless on a presentment or indictment of a grand jury, except in cases arising in the land or naval forces, or in the militia, when in actual service in time of war or public danger.

This provision applies only to the federal government. The Supreme Court has decided that the Fourteenth Amendment does not require the individual states to provide for indictment by a grand jury, provided the state affords some other mode of fair procedure. In *Hurtado* v. *California*[3] the Supreme Court approved of a practice which allowed prosecution for felony to be initiated by an "information"—i.e., a formal accusation by the public prosecutor—without indictment by a grand jury. The accused is examined before a local judge, who listens to the testimony. The attorney for the accused is present and is entitled to cross-examine the witnesses. The judge may then hand down an information setting forth those facts which satisfied him that there was reasonable basis for belief that the accused had perpetrated the crime.

A grand jury indictment is mandatory only in federal cases involving a "capital or otherwise infamous crime." Practically speaking, this means cases involving felonies, crimes punishable by death or imprisonment for more than one year.[4] When the crimes are within the jurisdiction of military authorities, grand jury indictment is not required, regardless of how serious the crime may be. The Fifth Amendment also expressly excludes "cases arising . . . in the militia, when in actual service in time of war or public danger." What this clause means in practice is that criminal cases which occur in the National Guard when it has been called into federal service are exempt from the provision of the Fifth Amendment which requires grand jury indictment.

The Constitution does not spell out how many people are needed in order to organize and conduct a grand jury or how these persons shall be selected. However, the implication of the Fifth Amendment is that the selection of the jurors shall be in such manner as to assure that any person accused of a serious crime will receive fair and just treatment. This requirement of fair treatment applies to the states in the same way that it binds the federal government. It follows that, while the state is not legally required to provide for a grand jury, if it does, the system of selection must be a just one. Thus, it cannot, as a matter of regular practice, exclude one segment of the population simply on the basis of race. When, in one case, it was shown that Negroes had been systematically kept off the grand jury which indicted two Negroes on charges of rape, the Supreme Court held that such exclusion had deprived the defendants of their right to due process of law.[5] This violated the Fourteenth Amendment. Of course, it almost goes without saying that, under the Fifth Amendment, such discriminatory exclusion may not be carried on by the federal government either.[6]

A grand jury does two important things. It decides whether there is sufficient evidence to hold an individual for trial on a specifically charged crime, and, by its indictment, it gives the accused notice of the crime with which he has been charged.

Usually, the district attorney or, perhaps, the police arrange for the appearance of witnesses and present evidence to the jury. The grand jury itself does have power to conduct its own investigation and to bring in its own witnesses, but, generally, it does not exercise this power.

When the finding of the grand jury is based on a showing made by the government prosecutor, it is termed an indictment. A determination stemming from an investigation started by the grand jury itself is called a presentment. The indictment is employed more frequently than the presentment.

In returning either an indictment or a presentment, the grand jury is required to carefully specify the elements of the crime which have allegedly been committed by the accused. Here technical or minor defects or irregularities do not invalidate the indictment, provided that the indictment clearly advises the defendant of the specific crime with which he has been charged. If the indictment fails to meet this requirement, it will be held invalid.[7]

DOUBLE JEOPARDY

The Anglo-American traditional sense of fair play recoils from the thought that a man who has been compelled to defend himself against criminal charges in one free trial might be made to defend himself again and again until, as a result of such persecution, he would ultimately be convicted. Based on this reasoning, a provision guarding against such harassment was incorporated into the Fifth Amendment:

> Nor shall any person be subject for the same offense to be twice put in jeopardy of life or limb.

This requirement is aimed only at the federal government. It does not specifically bind the states, and the double jeopardy provision has not been deemed extended to the states via the Fourteenth Amendment. However, the states are bound, under the Due Process Clause of the Fourteenth Amendment, to protect an individual from harassment and persecution in the administration of criminal charges. Thus, a state may technically try a person twice for the same offense; however, it may not arbitrarily persecute him.

A person who has been tried once for a crime has no guarantee that he will not have to go through the trial procedure again for the same crime. As a matter of fact, some persons have been subjected to trial several times for a single crime.[8]

As an example, if an accused person goes through an entire trial, is convicted, and, then, on his appeal it is discovered that there was some substantial error in the conduct of the trial, which deprived him of his rights or which might have resulted in an unjust conviction, the reviewing court may reverse the conviction. In so doing, the upper court is deciding that no correct trial has taken place, and, by ordering that the defendant be retried for the same crime, the appeal court is simply saying that the defendant should receive his first proper trial. In law this is simply considered part of the original jeopardy, not double jeopardy.

Double Jeopardy in the Federal Courts

If, after trial in a federal court, an accused person has been acquitted of one, or even all, of the charges brought against him, he is regarded as having been placed in jeopardy and may not be tried again under the same charges. Consistent with this philosophy, the law has long been clear that, under the Fifth Amendment, a verdict of acquittal is final and that this ends the jeopardy to which the defendant may be subjected.[9] It follows, therefore, that the United States attorney in the federal court cannot appeal a determination of "not guilty," although the accused is permitted to appeal a verdict of "guilty."

A person is considered in jeopardy as soon as his trial begins, when his liberty is threatened, even though he may not ultimately be found guilty. As a consequence, the prosecuting attorney may not commence a trial, and, once he feels that it is not going too well for the prosecution, stop the proceedings and initiate them again some other time. Yet, there are certain times when the facts or circumstances indicate that a particular trial is not or cannot or will not be fair to the defendant. When this happens, the court may declare a mistrial before the case has been submitted to the jury. A mistrial is appropriate when there is something about the conduct of the trial which is improper and, for this reason, the trial is vacated and a new trial ordered.

By way of illustration, if a trial had begun and, while it was in progress, one of the jurors reported that he had been offered a bribe to vote for acquittal, this would be a good basis for a mistrial. Under these circumstances, it would not be considered double jeopardy to subject the defendant to a new trial. However, once a jury has been sworn, it is not possible to declare a mistrial simply because the prosecution does not have all his witnesses available and ready to testify.

> Harassment of an accused by successive prosecutions or declaration of a mistrial so as to afford the prosecution more favorable opportunity to convict are examples when jeopardy attaches.[10]

Double Jeopardy in the State Courts

The states are not required to honor the "double jeopardy" provision of the federal Bill of Rights. However, some states have similar clauses in their own constitutions. In the historic case of *Palko* v. *Connecticut*[11] a local prosecutor appealed what he believed to be an erroneous decision. The defendant in this case had been charged and tried for murder in the first degree. However, the jury convicted him only of second degree murder, and the prosecutor asked for a reversal and appealed the decision. The decision was reversed, and, when the defendant was tried for the second time, the jury brought in a verdict of guilty of murder in the first degree. Then, the defendant appealed to the Supreme Court, arguing, among other things, that the Fifth Amendment applies to the states and that this second trial constituted double jeopardy. The Supreme Court decided that this portion of the Fifth Amendment does not restrict the states unless the circumstances are so shocking as to violate fundamental concepts of due process of law.

In a later case[12] a prosecutor asked a state court to declare a mistrial because two of his witnesses had not been able to appear. The court granted the mistrial because of this burden on the prosecutor, and the defendant was convicted. The defendant then took an appeal, arguing double jeopardy, to the Supreme Court of the United States. Again, the Supreme Court ruled that this provision of the Fifth Amendment was not binding to the states, and that the situation had not been so unfair as to violate the Fourteenth Amendment.

This decision points up the difference between the "due process" standard of the Fourteenth Amendment as applied to the states and the "double jeopardy" provision of the Fifth Amendment as applied to the federal government and its prosecutions. One thing that is quite clear is that, if a person is convicted and serves a sentence, the matter is ended there. If the state should attempt to try him again for the same crime because the prosecutor feels that the sentence was too lenient, it will undoubtedly be ruled a double jeopardy and illegal under the Due Process Clause.

REFUSAL TO ANSWER

The draftsmen of the Bill of Rights were very well acquainted with historic inquisitions based on torture, such as the infamous trials conducted by the Court of Star Chamber. Therefore, our Founding Fathers insisted upon inserting into the Bill of Rights a guarantee of protection against self-incrimination. This guarantee has been heralded by Dean Erwin Griswold of Harvard Law School as "one of the great landmarks in man's struggle to make himself civilized."

The Supreme Court has ruled that the clause of the Fifth Amendment which states that no person "shall be compelled in any criminal case to be a witness against himself" contains two basic ideas. The first is the right of a person to be protected against physical torture, coercion, or other attempts to force him to make a confession; the second is the right of a person to stand mute without inference of guilt being drawn from his silence. The first concept, protection from tortured confessions, is so fundamental to the idea of justice that it has long been considered part of the Fourteenth Amendment's guarantee of due process. As a result, neither the federal government nor the states may use force, duress, or coercion to extract confessions;[13]

and, since 1964, the right to stand mute, rather than speak and incriminate oneself, has also applied to the states as well as to the federal government.[14]

Forced Confessions

It is quite clear that confessions obtained by torture and physical torment are violative of the privilege against self-incrimination. "The rack and torture chamber may not be substituted for the witness stand."[15] In the case of *Brown* v. *Mississippi* a confession was thrown out because a sheriff who, encouraged and abetted by a mob, had horsewhipped the accused until he had finally broken down and confessed to the crime. Today, more subtle methods of duress or coercion may be employed, and they are more difficult to detect. While a free confession may be used against an individual, a confession resulting from coercion, whether psychological or physical, may vitiate it.

The Supreme Court set aside a confession in the case of *Leyra* v. *Denno*[16] because it had been obtained by a state-employed psychiatrist who had subjected the accused to an intense and very oppressing, searching interrogation. The doctor had been introduced to the suspect as a medical person who would be able to give him relief from a painful sinus condition.

In *Spano* v. *New York*[17] a friend of the accused had been called in by the New York police. They told this friend to inform the accused that, because he had helped the accused person, his job was threatened. This was not true; however, after being told this by his friend, the accused confessed to the crime. The Supreme Court decided that the sympathy which had been improperly aroused was a precipitating factor in bringing about the confession and, thus, the confession could not be employed to help convict the defendant.

In still another case[18] it was known that the defendant had been held by the police for long periods of time, and that he had not been given the opportunity to telephone a lawyer or his wife until he "cooperated." The Court said that this indicated "an atmosphere of substantial coercion and inducement," sufficient to vitiate the confession, even though no physical force had been used.

In 1966, in the landmark case of *Miranda* v. *Arizona*,[19] the Supreme Court underlined its intention of protecting accused persons from being forced to confess.

The Right to Stand Mute

In recent American history the right to stand mute has attracted a great deal of controversy and attention. This is the right of a defendant or a witness to refuse to testify on the grounds that it may tend to incriminate him. At the present time this right to refuse to testify is protected from deprivation by both the federal government and the states.

Criminal Trials

The defendant in a criminal case is not required to testify. In the federal courts neither the judge nor the government prosecutor may comment on the fact that the defendant chooses not to testify; nor is the jury permitted to draw any inference of guilt from this refusal. The logic of this rule is simply that, if it did not exist, a defendant who was entirely innocent of the crime could be forced to take the stand and reveal something from his past which would prejudice the jury against him.

Until recently, this rule did not apply in the state courts, and district attorneys and judges were permitted to advise the jury that they could draw their own conclusions from the refusal of the defendant to testify. The defendant, therefore, either had to testify or else to take a chance that the jury might decide he was guilty because he didn't testify.[20] In 1964 the U.S. Supreme Court overruled the cases so holding.[21] Today, in state courts, just as in the federal courts, neither the prosecutor nor the judge may comment on the failure of the defendant to take the stand in his own behalf.[22]

Other Proceedings

While the constitutional amendment protecting the privilege against self-incrimination applies expressly to "criminal cases," the law is clear that the privilege also covers persons testifying in other proceedings who might be incriminated if they were compelled to answer certain questions under oath. This privilege against self-incrimination applies to witnesses who are asked to testify before legislative committees.[23] The reason for this is that an answer before a congressional committee might lead to prosecution, even though Congress itself is not a court and cannot prosecute.

Likewise, a person who is called to testify before a grand jury may refuse to give any information that might serve to incriminate him. However, he must take the stand, and he must specifically invoke his privilege against self-incrimination. He may even decline to answer those questions which would only indirectly tend to incriminate him. He may also refuse to answer if what he says might provide a "link in the chain" of incriminating evidence.[24]

As an example, a person on the witness stand may refuse to say whether he and John Smith were partners in an armed robbery. He may also refuse to answer a much more simple question, whether he saw John Smith on the night in question, if the answer to this seemingly innocuous querry could lead to other more incriminating questions and answers.

Immunity Statutes

We have seen that a person testifying under oath may refuse to answer if what he says might result in a criminal prosecution against him. However, suppose that he were guaranteed in advance of his testimony that he could not be prosecuted on the basis of his answers. The Supreme Court has decided that, if a statute gives the person testifying immunity from prosecution resulting from his testimony, he no longer has the right to remain silent. Once the accused or witness is given an immunity from prosecution, he must testify and cannot invoke the Fifth Amendment.[25]

At one time the court held that, even if the immunity did not cover all possible prosecution from every source, the testimony could not be refused. A witness could be compelled to testify in a federal trial, although his answers might be the basis for prosecution in a state proceeding. He could be required to testify in a state court, even though he could still be prosecuted federally. At the present time, however, the law is settled that the immunity must be sufficient to protect the witness from more prosecution resulting from his testimony before he can be compelled to answer:

> We hold that the constitutional privilege against self-incrimination protects a state witness against incrimination under federal, as well as state, law, and a federal witness against discrimination under state, as well as federal law.[26]

In two cases the Supreme Court recently spelled out the law to be applied to city employees who refuse to waive the privilege or to testify. One case involved a New York City patrolman who was subpoened to appear to testify before a grand jury investigating bribery. He was advised that, if he did not sign a waiver of immunity, he would be dismissed. He was fired when he refused to sign the waiver.[27] The other case centered around the New York City Commissioner of Investigation, who, while investigating reports that employees of the Department of Sanitation were pocketing fees that should have gone to the city, summoned fifteen employees and advised them that, if they refused to testify about their conduct or that of other city employees, they would be dismissed. Twelve of them refused to testify and were dismissed for that reason. Three testified, but when they were called before the grand jury they refused to sign waivers of immunity, so they were fired, too. The Supreme Court ruled in both cases that the dismissals were improper since public employees, like all other persons, are entitled to the constitutional privilege against self-incrimination.[28]

At the same time, the Court upheld the disqualification of a corporation from obtaining public contracts because of a company officer's refusal to waive immunity in an investigation of bid rigging.[29] The privilege against self-incrimination, said the Court, is essentially a personal privilege and cannot be resorted to by a corporation.

DUE PROCESS OF LAW

Chapter 29 of the Magna Carta provided:

> No free man shall be taken and imprisoned or disseized or exiled or in any way destroyed nor will we go upon him or decend upon him except by lawful judgment of his peers and by the law of the land.

Sir William Blackstone once said that this provision, which was extracted by the bishops and barons of England from King John in 1215, was itself enough justification for the name Great Charter.

A long time ago the phrase "law of the land" was defined by Sir Edward Coke as meaning the same as "due process of law." These two phrases were used almost interchangeably in the colonial constitutions and the early American charters. When the original Bill of Rights was propounded, this concept of "the law of the land" or "due process of law" was incorporated into the Fifth Amendment:

> Nor shall any person . . . be deprived of life, liberty or property, without due process of law.

This guarantee set out in the Fifth Amendment binds only the federal government. There is a separate Due Process Clause in the Fourteenth Amendment and this binds the states.

The Nature of Due Process of Law

It is impossible to detail with specificity the various attributes and applications of the Bill of Rights. In describing the nature of "due process of law," a Supreme Court justice once said, "Due process of law is a summarized constitutional guaranty of respect for those personal immunities which . . . are 'so rooted in the traditions and conscience of our people as to be ranked as fundamental' . . ."[30]

The Due Process Clause is sometimes regarded as having two aspects, one substantive and the other procedural. Generally speaking, "substantive due process" refers to that which prohibits laws because they are unfair in their content, and "procedural due process" refers to that which prohibits unfair methods of applying the law in a given situation. For example, a federal law which required all redheaded, freckle-faced school teachers to pay twice as much income tax as other taxpayers would clearly be a denial of substantive due process because it is unfair in content. Procedural due process would be violated, on the other hand, if the tax law itself were fair, but all the redheaded, freckle-faced teachers were given ten years imprisonment for alleged failure to pay this tax, without having had a trial or hearing.

The principles of "due process of law" control all the processings of government. "Due process" is a restriction on Congress and prohibits its members from arbitrary exercise of their lawmaking authority.

This does not mean that Congress cannot make laws which have different impacts on different groups of people or which apply only to certain groups of people. Congress can certainly regulate the conduct of federal employees, even though the same rules do not apply to other citizens or other workers. It can regulate the railroads in a different manner from the way in which it regulates the national banks. Reasonable classification is certainly permitted under the "due process" provision. What is prohibited is making "arbitrary, unreasonable or capricious" laws. As the Supreme Court once said, the essential element of due process is that it "bars Congress from enactments that shock the sense of fair play."[31]

The Due Process Clause restricts the executive branch of government, just as it restricts Congress. When the executive exercises a lawmaking or rule-making function, he is required to adhere to due process of law and is not permitted to make rules which are unreasonable or arbitrary.

Procedural due process makes it mandatory that the laws are applied in a fair and equal manner. A long time ago, in discussing the concept of the "law of the land," Daniel Webster explained:

> By the law of the land, it is most clearly intended that general law; a law which heretofore had condemned; which proceeds upon inquiry and renders judgment only after trial. The meaning is that every citizen shall hold his life, liberty, property and immunities, under the protection of the general rules which govern society.[32]

It is not possible to spell out all the situations to which "due process" applies or to describe all the cases which must be considered.

Basic to our philosophy of government is the idea that every person has the right to tell his side of the story before the government can deprive him of his life, liberty, or his property, and that he has a right to be fairly heard. This is the essential meaning of "due process."

The Expanding Scope of Due Process of Law

In a number of cases decided within the last decade the Supreme Court has recognized the right to travel abroad as part of the liberty of which citizens cannot be deprived without due process of law under the Fifth Amendment. It is held that such a right may not be limited because of the political beliefs of a citizen or because of his associations, but only in order to protect our national security.[33]

It is interesting to note that, in the Aptheker case,[34] Justice Goldberg attempted to apply the preferred freedoms concept, which has been used with respect to First Amendment cases, to the right of foreign travel, which was held to be a part of liberty implicit in the Fifth Amendment. The Justice stated that he felt travel involves freedoms that are delicate and vulnerable as well as supremely precious in our society. And he added, "Since freedom of travel is a constitutional liberty closely related to the rights of free speech and association, I believe that the appellants in this case should be required to assume the burden of demonstrating that Congress could not have written the statute constitutionally prohibiting their travel."

However, the right to travel abroad is not an absolute right. It can be limited when considerations of foreign policy or national security justify it.[35]

In another extraordinary case[36] the Court invalidated the 1879 Connecticut statute which made it a punishable offense for "any person" to advise or give a device "for the purpose of preventing contraception." A great many people could have been accused of violating this law since another Connecticut statute states that any person who assists, abets, or causes anyone to commit an offense "may be prosecuted and punished as if he were the principal offender."

In this case the Court referred to the right of "marital privacy" implicit in "several provisions of the Constitution, such as, for example, the First, Fourth and Fifth Amendments."

It seems clear that the scope of the Fifth Amendment, like that of the First Amendment, is being expanded to include more and more personal rights enjoyed by citizens and to protect them under the Constitution.

THE RIGHT TO JUST COMPENSATION FOR PROPERTY

One of the rights guaranteed by the Magna Carta, Chapter 29, was that "no free man shall be . . . disseized . . . except . . . by the law of the land." Simply stated, this meant that the Crown could not take property away from individuals unless it did so pursuant to the provisions of the law. Implied in this guarantee is the concept that when property is taken, it should be paid for on a fair basis. These concepts were set forth in the Fifth Amendment as follows:

> Nor shall private property be taken for public use, without just compensation.

In 1833 the Supreme Court of the United States declared that this provision of the Fifth Amendment restricted the federal government and not the individual states.[37] Once the Fourteenth Amendment was adopted, however, the Supreme Court ruled that it applied to the states and that they were required to pay just compensation for property taken by them.[38]

The Purpose of Taking Property

As the language of the amendment indicates, the property which is taken must be for "public use." It cannot be taken arbitrarily, but only for a legitimate public enterprise. Usually, once the legislature determines what the use is to be and that this constitutes a valid public purpose, the courts give this exercise of discretion considerable weight:

> It is the function of Congress to decide what type of taking is for public use. . . . When Congress has spoken on this subject "its decision is entitled to deference until it is shown to involve an impossibility.". . . Any departure from this judicial restraint would result in Courts deciding on what is and what is not a government function and in their invalidating legislation on the basis of their view on that question at the moment of decision.[39]

Thus, as a general rule, the courts will not substitute their own opinions as to whether or not the purpose is a valid public one for those of the legislature.[40] At the same time, the courts are obligated not to uphold an arbitrary grant of property for purposes which are not public. In recent years the concept of "public purpose" seems to be more and more attenuated.

The Procedure of Taking

The Fifth Amendment does not set out any specific techniques or procedures for acquiring property. However, the Due Process Clauses of both the Fifth and Fourteenth Amendments do apply to the taking of private property. The courts have ruled that this application of "due process" entitles the owner of property which is to be seized to a hearing during which he may present his objections.[41]

With the extension of public use of property, it is quite common to read newspaper accounts of objections raised by private property owners who appeared in court to argue against the construction of a federal road or urban renewal project on their property. Such hearings are predicated on the protection established by the Fifth Amendment.

Payment of Just Compensation

The Fifth Amendment provides that private property cannot be taken by the government for public use "without just compensation."

> Fifth Amendment's guarantee that private property shall not be taken for public use without just compensation was designed to bar government from forcing some people alone to bear public burdens which, in all fairness and justice, should be borne by the public as a whole.[42]

Court proceedings called "condemnation proceedings" have been provided by law to ensure that there are regular hearings at which the compensation mandated by the Fifth Amendment will be determined on a proper basis and paid as a matter of due course. The computation of what is considered to be "just" is determined by the court on the basis of a fair evaluation of the value of the property in question.[43]

8. Fair Trials in Criminal and Civil Cases

AMENDMENTS VI, VII and VIII

AMONG THE grievances which were enumerated against George III of England in the Declaration of Independence was the complaint that he had, in many cases, withheld from his colonial subjects "the benefits of trial by jury." The colonists regarded trial by jury as such a fundamental right that the original Constitution included this procedural protection in Article III, Section 2 and, later, to underscore its importance, they inserted it into the Bill of Rights. Amendment Six covered the assurance of trial by jury in criminal prosecutions. It provided:

> In all criminal prosecutions, the accused shall enjoy the right to a speedy and public trial, by an impartial jury of the state and district wherein the crime shall have been committed, which district shall have been previously ascertained by law, and to be informed of the nature and cause of the accusation; to be confronted with the witnesses against him; to have compulsory process for obtaining witnesses in his favor, and to have the assistance of counsel for his defense.

FAIR TRIAL IN CRIMINAL CASES

The Right to Trial by Jury

On May 20, 1968, the Supreme Court announced its decisions in a number of criminal cases that are destined to revolutionize criminal procedure and substantive law in the United States.

The most significant of the five rulings was *Duncan* v. *Louisiana*,[1] in which the Court followed a trend established by several recent cases that have made various provisions of the Bill of Rights binding on the states, even though they originally included only the federal government. In the Duncan case the Court ruled that the states are bound by the Sixth Amendment's requirement of jury trial in criminal cases.

In 1900 the High Court held that a state jury of less than twelve members is permissible because the Sixth Amendment applied only to federal trials. Since then the states have been considered free to work out their own jury procedures.

All states guarantee jury trials in serious cases, but there have been many variations which deviate from the federal standards. Under the Duncan ruling, jury trials are considered so basic to the American system of a fair trial that they are deemed mandatory in state criminal cases by the provision in the Fourteenth Amendment that prohibits states from denying individuals the right to life or liberty without due process of law.

Justice White, speaking for a majority of eight, noted that the so-called "petty offenses" have traditionally been tried without a right to trial by jury. He pointed out that this practice would be continued. The line between "serious" and "petty" cases was not drawn but was left for future decisions. The precise case before the court was considered a serious one. It involved Gary Duncan, a black youth who was charged with simple battery after he pushed or touched a white youth. Duncan was trying to prevent a fight which appeared imminent between white and black boys. His request for a jury trial was denied, and he was convicted and sentenced to sixty days in jail and fined $150. The decision may make mandatory a tremendous expansion of the system of criminal administration.[2] For instance, in New York, jury trials have not been available up to now in misdemeanor cases which may carry jail terms of up to one year.

Even when the accused does have a right to have the charges against him heard by a jury, he may waive this right if he feels that a trial by a judge sitting alone, rather than by a jury, will best serve his interests. However, both the government and the judge, as well as the defendant, must consent to this waiver.[3] It seems noteworthy that a defendant does not have a constitutional right to have a trial without a jury.[4]

Speedy and Public Trial

The requirement of a speedy and public trial is an almost direct result of the early colonists' experiences with the secret inquisitions and drawn-out interrogations of the Old World. The Founding Fathers sought to assure the defendant that every effort would be made to locate the witnesses and to find the evidence while it was still available. There is no fixed amount of time that constitutes such an unreasonable delay as to deprive the accused of his "speedy" trial and, therefore, entitle him to a dismissal of the charges. In a case growing out of World War II, a federal court dismissed an indictment for treason against a man who was charged with working with the Japanese, because he was held for six years before his trial.[5]

The High Court has decided that the Due Process Clause of the Fourteenth Amendment mandates a public trial in the state courts, just as the Sixth Amendment requires it in the federal courts. In one case a pinball machine operator was subpoened, under a Michigan statute to come before a judge who was conducting an investigation into gambling. The judge thought that the man's testimony was false and, therefore, held him in contempt. The determination of perjury was based on evidence which was not disclosed by the court. The Supreme Court reversed the conviction, stating that the defendant could not be tried and convicted on the basis of undisclosed information.[6]

There is considerable agitation today over the extent to which a trial judge can regulate the people who attend a courtroom trial.

This is illustrated by the famous trial involving Billy Sol Estes. Even before the trial began, there had been a tremendous amount of publicity devoted to the story. Volume after volume had been filled with press clippings and photographs. A hearing before the trial had been televised and carried "live" on radio. A dozen cameramen, at least, were present at the hearing. Electronic equipment, cables, and wires were snaked out across the floor of the courtroom. The judge's bench was encrusted with many microphones, and still others were planted at the jury box and at the tables of the attorneys involved. By the time the trial was ready to open, the court had ordered a booth constructed for the purpose of containing the cameramen. "Live" coverage of the actual trial was restricted to the opening statements of the attorneys and the summation of the prosecutor. However, films and video tapes without sound were taken all during the trial.

In his appeal the defendant argued that the televising of his trial, as well as other widespread publicity, had prevented him from receiving a fair hearing in accordance with due process of law. Considering this background, the Supreme Court decided that, in spite of the restrictions which had been imposed during the trial, the televising of the trial under the conditions described had breached the constitutional rights of Mr. Estes.[7]

Impartial Jury

An impartial jury should represent a cross section of the community. What this means is that no group should be systematically excluded from jury duty. Thus, a policy of excluding Negroes or daily wage earners is prejudicial.[8] Yet, compare with these rulings the one involving a Florida law which compelled men to serve on juries but only allowed women who actually volunteered. A woman who was convicted by a jury consisting only of men challenged the law, and the Court held that due process of law had not been violated.

Trial Where Crime Was Committed

One of the complaints included in the Declaration of Independence was that, under English rule, Americans had been "transported beyond the seas" to be tried far from their native shores. The draftsmen of the Bill of Rights believed that a person should have the right to be tried where the crime had been committed in order to make it easier for him to find witnesses and so that any other evidence he might need would be readily available.

The Sixth Amendment orders that a person be tried by "an impartial jury of the State and district wherein the crime shall have been committed, which district shall have been previously ascertained by law."

In a recent decision[9] the Supreme Court ruled that jurors cannot be excluded automatically simply because they object to capital punishment.

William Witherspoon was convicted and sentenced to death by an Illinois jury for killing a Chicago policeman in 1959. Any venireman who objected to capital punishment had been excluded from serving on the jury, as a matter of course. By a vote of six to three the High Court held that such procedure violated the right of the defendant to a representative jury.

The Court said that the defendant had not been tried by a true cross section of the community, since, according to an established poll, only forty-two percent of the nation favors the death penalty. "Whatever else might be said of capital punishment, it is at least clear that its imposition by a hanging jury cannot be squared with the Constitution," wrote Justice Potter Stewart. The Court, however, still permits states to exclude from juries those persons who admit under questioning that their opposition to the death sentence is so strong that they could never vote to execute a defendant or even bring in a verdict of guilty.

The rationale of the Court is that it is all right to exclude a venireman who would refuse to vote for the death penalty under any circumstances. But a person cannot be eliminated simply because he has scruples against capital punishment. A jury that automatically excludes a large percentage of the population is unfairly weighed. Therefore, any defendant who has been sentenced by a jury so selected must now be sentenced again. However, the Court made it clear that convictions by the original juries could not be set aside simply on that ground.

Hugo Black argued that such logic was based on "semantic camouflage." Juries with members who are predisposed against the death sentence "will seldom if ever vote to impose the death penalty. This is just human nature. If this court is to hold capital punishment unconstitutional, it should do so forthrightly, not by making it impossible for the states to get juries that that the district where the trial is to be held "shall have been previously ascertained by law," Congress has set up the districts in which crime shall be tried. The district from which the jury is taken and where the trial is held is known as the "venue."

It is not always easy to decide the venue for a trial. For instance, in a case involving not only a criminal act, but also a conspiracy among the participants,[10] the Supreme Court held that the trial should be heard where the act took place, rather than where the conspiracy began. In another case,[11] a number of conscientious objectors refused to report to a hospital in which the Selective Service authorities had ordered them to do non-military work. The Court decided that they should be tried in the area where the hospital was located, although they had refused to report at another place.

Obviously, however, the prosecutor cannot be permitted to pick the place for trial simply because it seems most favorable for the prosecution's case. Thus, when an official of a union filed a false report with the National Labor Relations Board in Washington, D.C., it was decided that the crime occurred in Washington where the report was filed, not in Colorado where it was mailed. For that reason, the defendant could not be tried in Colorado, although the prosecutor sought to have the case tried there.[12]

To date, the Supreme Court has not answered the question of whether or not the Due Process Clause of the Fourteenth Amendment dictates to the states in deciding where the trial may be held.

The Right to Be Informed of Charges and to Face Accusers

It is clear law that an accused person, in order to properly defend himself, is given the right to be informed of the charges lodged against him. A person accused of a criminal act has the right to confront his accusers when he is being tried. He is certainly entitled to be present in the courtroom at the time they testify against him, and he has the right to cross-examine them.

This right to confront one's accusers operates in both federal and state trials. In one case[13] a man had no attorney when he came before a judge in a preliminary hearing. The chief witness against him was examined by the prosecuting attorney, but the defendant did not cross-examine him. By the time the trial came about, this principal witness had relocated in California. However, the court permitted the attorney for the prosecution to introduce a transcript of the main witness's earlier testimony. The Supreme Court of the United States set aside the defendant's conviction because he had been denied the right to confront and cross-examine the principal witness against him. The Court also held, in another case,[14] that the defendant had been denied the right to confront his accuser. In this case the confession of an accomplice in the crime was read to the jury. However, the defendant could not cross-examine the accomplice concerning the truth of the confession.

Except in unusual circumstances, an accused person has the right to confront and cross-examine those persons who testify against him. An example of such exception might occur when a person has been tried and convicted of a crime, and, then, his conviction is reversed. The testimony offered against him at the first trial may be introduced against him again, even though the witness is dead and, thus, cannot be cross-examined at the second trial. This testimony is permissible because, at the first trial, the accused person did have an opportunity to cross-examine. There are other exceptions, as well, but the above example gives some indication as to how they work.

The Right to Subpoena Witnesses

Obviously, an accused person is entitled to have witnesses appear and testify in his behalf if they want to. Moreover, under the Sixth Amendment, he is also entitled to some process by which the Court can compel witnesses to appear and testify, even if they are unwilling to do so. While some question may exist as to the exact scope of this right, it is clear that not permitting the accused person to subpoena witnesses to testify in his behalf violates the constitutional guaranty of due process of law and a fair trial. This is also probably an accurate statement of the law as it applies to the state courts under the Due Process Clause of the Fourteenth Amendment. However, the right is not unlimited—even in the federal courts, there is no unrestricted right to subpoena witnesses.

For example, in one case,[15] the accused had been examined by a team of psychiatrists at a government hospital. One of the psychiatrists testified for the government as to the results of the examination. The Sixth Amendment did not give the accused a right to subpoena the other two doctors, especially since the United States was paying for transportation and other expenses.

The Right to Counsel

Under the common law of old England, a person accused of a felony had to rely on the judge who, in effect, served as his counsel at his trial. The accused had no independent right to counsel. This was also the law in the American Colonies until the Bill of Rights was adopted.

The Sixth Amendment insures the right to counsel, and it has been held that this right is absolute in the federal courts. Originally, the Sixth Amendment, with its right to counsel, restricted only the federal government. Of course, since the famous case of *Gideon* v. *Wainright*,[16] this right has also applied to the states. In the Gideon case a prisoner sought release from prison on the grounds that he had been denied the help of an attorney at his trial. His contention was that this violated his rights under the Sixth and Fourteenth Amendments. Since he had been unable to hire a lawyer, he had asked the state court to appoint one to represent him. The Florida court had failed to do so, saying that, under the laws of the state, counsel appointed by the court was available only in capital cases. Inasmuch as Gideon had been charged with breaking and entering, a non-capital felony, he was not entitled to have counsel appointed under the law of the state. Gideon defended himself and subsequently was convicted. The Supreme Court pointed out that the Due Process Clause of the Fourteenth Amendment included the right to counsel and added, "In our adversary system of criminal justice, any person hailed into Court, who is too poor to hire a lawyer, cannot be assured a fair trial unless counsel is provided for him."

Thus, the law is clear that a person who is tried either in the federal or state courts is entitled to be represented by counsel. Nor is this right to counsel restricted to the trial itself. Frequently, it is more important to have the assistance of counsel before the trial.[17]

In *Escobito v. Illinois*,[18] the defendant was arrested without a warrant in connection with the shooting of his brother. His own lawyer obtained his release. Eleven days later another suspect made incriminatory statements against Escobito, and he was once more arrested and brought to police headquarters. While being questioned by the police, he made several attempts to talk to his lawyer, but these requests were denied or ignored. In the interim, his lawyer had arrived at police headquarters, and he also made several requests to see Escobito. However, these, too, were ignored. The lawyer stayed at police headquarters for over three hours without being permitted to talk to his client. After an extensive interrogation Escobito made some incriminating statements, and these statements were used against him at the trial.

When the case came before the Supreme Court, Escobito's conviction was reversed. Therefore, today, neither the federal nor the state government may deny an individual who is charged with a crime his right to counsel. This right may arise at a very preliminary stage, long before the trial itself. In addition, the accused person who is too impecunious to hire a lawyer to protect his rights is entitled to have one appointed by the court for the purpose of trial or earlier in the proceeding. These principles have been heavily underscored by the Miranda case.[19]

TRIAL BY JURY IN CIVIL CASES

Article III, Section 2 of the Constitution provided for trial by jury in criminal cases. Although some of the men at the Constitutional Convention favored a provision which would also establish trial by jury in civil cases, such a clause was never drafted into the body of the Constitution. At the time of the Constitutional Convention the colonists were used to trial by jury in civil cases, just as in criminal cases, in keeping with the established procedure in England. However, when the Bill of Rights was being formulated, someone advanced the idea that a guaranty of a jury trial in civil cases be included, and the recommendation was adopted as the Seventh Amendment:

> In suits at common law, where the value in controversy shall exceed twenty dollars, the right of trial by jury shall be preserved, and no fact tried by a jury shall be otherwise reexamined in any court of the United States, than according to the rules of the common law.

This provision is applicable only to cases being tried in the federal courts. It does not bind the states, and the states are not compelled to provide a jury trial in civil cases unless their own constitutions impose such a rule.[20]

The Common Law Right to Jury Trial

The Seventh Amendment gives a litigant the right to a jury trial under the same circumstances and in the same manner as in the rules of the common law. In the early days of English common law certain specific forms of action were believed to be sufficient to protect all personal rights which fell within the jurisdiction of the courts. Before the courts could listen to a case, the complainant had to bring an action which would fit one of the established forms. The recognized claims included an action, based upon breach of contract, for the recovery of money; action for the recovery of specific property; action for the recovery of money damages due to injury to personal property; and action for an accounting of money concerning the administration of property. For a short span of time the aggrieved party had no remedy for his claim unless he could make his case fit into one of the established forms of action. These forms, plus a few others which were later approved, were the only suits permitted at common law; and these were the cases heard by a jury.

Because these available forms of action were so rigid and restricted, a parallel system developed along with the common law. This was called "equity," and the underlying approach was an appeal, based on conscience and justice, to the Crown for special help. Since these equity claims were direct appeals to the king's mercy and instinct, there was no right or need for a trial by jury.

At the present time, in the federal courts, the separation once made between the courts of equity and the courts of law no longer exists. The rigid forms of action have been done away with. In spite of this, however, a distinction is still made between those cases based on legal principles and those cases based on equitable ones. It is only in the cases at law that the right to jury is guaranteed. These are roughly predicated upon the same theories that they were in the days when feudalism was breaking down. Broadly speaking, they include cases involving contracts, damage to property, debts, and personal injuries.

Thus, there is no right to trial by jury in cases involving equity jurisdiction. Furthermore, there is no right to trial by jury in actions brought against the government, which stands in the shoes of the Crown. In England cases concerning the law of the sea, or admiralty, were handled by separate courts, rather than by the traditional common law courts. For this reason there is no right to trial by jury in such actions. Also, when a lawsuit is based on a new right created by an act of Congress, as opposed to a right established at common law, the right to jury does not exist.[21] In addition, the right to jury trial does not exist with respect to small claims "where the value in controversy does not exceed twenty dollars."

Where there is a right to a jury trial in the federal court system, it is a right to a jury as conceived of at common law. This means that the jury must consist of twelve people and that, to be effective, the verdict, must be the unanimous decision of these twelve.[22]

Since state courts are not restricted by the Seventh Amendment, they do not have to provide for jury trials, or they may provide for smaller juries or for a majority, rather than a unanimous, verdict. It should be kept in mind that, under the Seventh Amendment, jury trial may be waived by the parties involved.

The Job of the Jury

Every lawsuit involves a dispute over the law to be applied, the actual facts in controversy, or both the law and the facts. Obviously, if the parties did not have a disagreement, no suit would have been instituted. What is involved in most cases is the application of either a statute or a judge-made law to a set of facts. It is the task of the judge to formulate the principles of law which may be applicable and to make the jury aware of these rules. It is the job of the jury to resolve disputes over questions of fact and to apply the appropriate principles of law to them.

For example, A sues B on the grounds that B was driving in a negligent manner when he failed to observe a stop sign and, as a result, collided with A's car. A claims that he was careful, but B simply went through the stop sign without looking. The judge decides that, under the law, A may recover for his property damages and personal injuries if B was negligent and

A himself was free from contributory negligence. He tells the jury that, if A was negligent or if both of them were, A cannot recover. It is the jury's job to decide whether, in fact, A was negligent, B was negligent, or both of them were negligent actors.

Most cases involve questions of both law and fact. However, the parties may reach an agreement as to the facts, and, therefore, no question with respect to the facts is left for the jury. When this happens, the requirement of jury trial no longer exists. At other times, the evidence presented for one side is so strong, and the evidence presented for the other is so weak that reasonable men could only decide one way in reaching a verdict. In these cases the judge may direct the jury to give a verdict for the party who has made the strong showing. This does not violate the Seventh Amendment.[23]

Under the Seventh Amendment no appellate court can reverse a jury's determination of facts, its verdict, "otherwise . . . than according to the rules of common law." Yet, there are times when a jury's verdict could be set aside under the common law; and, thus, the jury's verdict may also be set aside in some instances under the Seventh Amendment.

It may happen that the judge is convinced there is only one possible decision the jury could reach, but, for some reason, he doesn't direct a verdict. Or the judge may misconstrue the facts and believe that more than one decision is possible as a reasonable response to the evidence; and, therefore, he may incorrectly fail to direct a verdict. If under these circumstances the jury should reach a decision which the judge considers unreasonable, the judge may then set the returned verdict aside on the grounds that there should have been a directed verdict in the first place.

When the trial judge should have directed a certain verdict and the verdict which the jury found is considered to be unreasonable, it may also be set aside by an appeal court. This is permitted under the Seventh Amendment because it was permissible at common law.[24]

A jury verdict may be set aside under other circumstances. If the jury actually has been deceived, the verdict may be considered invalid. For example, if perjury has been committed with respect to a material matter of evidence, the jury's verdict may be set aside and a new trial ordered. Likewise, if the judge stated the law incorrectly in his instructions to the jury, or if the law which was explained to the jury was incorrect, the verdict may be set aside.[25]

To paraphrase the requirement of the Seventh Amendment, a jury trial is guaranteed in federal civil cases if the amount in dispute is more than twenty dollars and if the action is of the type that was heard by a jury at common law. The verdict of the jury is final except when such determination could have been set aside at common law.

REASONABLE BAIL AND FAIR PUNISHMENT

Laws which forbade both excessive bail and cruel and unusual punishment were passed by Parliament in England in 1553 and again in 1668. The constitutions of a number of colonies contained similar safeguards. Thus, when the United States Constitution and, later, the Bill of Rights were drafted and adopted, the right to reasonable bail and the right to be protected from cruel and unusual punishment were firmly established on this continent. It is not surprising, as a consequence, that prohibitions against excessive bail and also against cruel and unusual punishment were included in the Bill of Rights:

> Excessive bail shall not be required, nor excessive fines imposed, nor cruel and unusual punishments inflicted.

Until recently the Eighth Amendment had not received too much attention from the courts. The question of whether or not the Eighth Amendment's provisions have been applied to the states through the Fourteenth Amendment is still not entirely settled. A number of early cases had held that the "excessive bail" provision did not apply to the states. However, in 1963, a circuit court of appeals stated, "We take it for granted that contrary to early cases . . . the prohibition in the Eighth Amendment against requiring excessive bail must now be regarded as applying to the states, under the Fourteenth Amendment."[26] The Supreme Court itself has not ruled on this issue.

Likewise, early cases had held that the Eighth Amendment's provision prohibiting cruel and unusual punishment did not apply to the states. However, in a decision announced in 1962,[27] the Supreme Court indicated that this protection is part of the Fourteenth Amendment and is applicable to the states. A number of recent cases have applied that decision.[28]

If the provisions prohibiting excessive bail and forbidding cruel and unusual punishment are extended to the states through the "due process of law" provision of the Fourteenth Amendment, it is logical to assume that the prohibition of excessive fines is included as well. However, this, too, has not been definitely settled by the High Court.

Prohibition of Excessive Bail

A person who has been arrested and charged with a crime often is not tried for a considerable time after his arrest, possibly weeks or months. Bail is a device designed to make sure that, at the time of trial, the defendant will show up in court. Permitting an arrested person to post bail protects him from having to remain in custody until the date of trial. The defendant agrees that, if he doesn't appear for trial on the specified day, he will forfeit property or money. The property or money required for bail is generally fixed by the judge who has committed the arrested person to custody.

As a matter of practice, it is not always the property or money of the accused person that is furnished as bail. There are professional people, called bail bondsmen, who supply the bail as a form of insurance. They put up the required amount and charge the accused person a certain premium to pay for this service.

The Eighth Amendment does not say that every accused person is entitled to be released if he is willing to put up bail. Usually, the statutes distinguish and define offenses which are "bailable" and those which are not. Bail is generally not available to those charged with military crimes or to those accused of murder or other capital offenses.[29]

If the accused is entitled to bail under the law, the Eighth Amendment prescribes that the amount of bail shall not be "excessive." The amount of bail is determined on the basis of the facts and circumstances of each case. In fixing bail the courts often consider such things as the ability of the accused to raise the bail, the nature of the crime, the character of the accused, and the accused's reputation in the community in which he lives.

As an example, a person who has been a multiple offender and who has previously shown himself to be irresponsible in returning to face trial might be required to post higher bail than someone who has been arrested for the first time and has a good reputation among his neighbors. There is no monetary formula for deciding what constitutes excessive bail. To a wealthy man charged with a "white collar crime" a hundred dollars might simply be the cost of an evening on the town, while to an impecunious defendant it could represent an unattainable fortune.

In *Stack* v. *Boyle*[30] the Supreme Court decided that the requirement of $50,000 bail for violation of the Smith Act regarding Communist conspiracy was too much. The High Court said that, when the local court fixes bail, it must be able to justify the amount.

Prohibition of Excessive Fines

Just as it did with bail requirements, the Supreme Court decided in the early part of the last century that the prohibition against excessive fines restricted the federal courts. However, it would not review the fines imposed by state courts, even though, in many cases, these fines appeared to be much too high.[31]

As a result, there aren't many federal cases which analyze the nature of excessive fines or indicate the standards to be used in deciding whether or not a fine is excessive. Actually, it has been left to Congress to set limits for fines and to trial courts to use their discretion and decide what fines should be levied in a particular case.

Prohibition of Cruel and Unusual Punishment

Although the issue of what constitutes "cruel and unusual punishment" has been before the courts many times, it is very difficult to promulgate an adequate and fixed definition. Obviously, as long as society is in a constant state of change, the nature of the crime, the particular facts and circumstances of the case, and the sanctions which have traditionally been employed will help determine whether a particular punishment is cruel and unusual.

In a fairly recent case[32] a sentence of a three year prison term plus twenty lashes for grand larceny was not considered by a state court to be a violation of the Eighth Amendment. However, a statute that authorized twelve to twenty years imprisonment plus a fine for "entry of known false statements in the public record" was deemed to be invalid by the Supreme Court on the grounds that the penalty was so out of proportion to the crime as to constitute a cruel and unusual punishment.[33] The Supreme

Court has decided that a California statute which punished narcotics addiction as a crime called for a punishment which was cruel and unusual.[34] The majority of the justices concluded, "In the light of contemporary knowledge, law which made a criminal offense of such a disease would doubtless be universally thought to be an infliction of cruel and unusual punishment in violation of the Eighth and Fourteenth Amendments." Compare with this view the ruling that prison is an appropriate punishment for intoxication.[35]

Punishment which is considered cruel and unusual does not always involve physical suffering. In *Trop* v. *Dulles*[36] the Supreme Court decided that loss of citizenship as punishment for wartime desertion from the military was cruel and unusual and, hence, was forbidden by the Eighth Amendment.

According to decided cases, death is not a cruel and unusual penalty, no matter whether it is executed by shooting,[37] or by deadly gas,[38] or in one of several other ways.

In 1947 a man named Francis was convicted of murder in Louisiana and sentenced to death. The electric chair was brought to the local jail for carrying out the sentence. On the day set for the execution, Francis was strapped into the chair. The switch was pulled, and Francis was "executed." But the current did not kill him. It did not even injure him seriously. A new warrant was issued for his execution. It was argued on his behalf that it would be cruel and unusual punishment to execute him twice for the same crime. Four of the Supreme Court judges assumed "without deciding" that the Eighth Amendment applied to the state, but, under the circumstances of the case, they did not feel that the second execution would be cruel and unusual. Another justice indicated his belief that the Eighth Amendment did not apply to the states but that the Due Process Clause of the Fourteenth Amendment could bar cruel and unusual punishments. However, this justice did not regard the second execution as a violation of due process. Four dissenting judges described the case as "death by installments." They thought that the second execution should be barred by the Eighth and Fourteenth Amendments.[39] Ultimately, Francis was executed.

The Eighth Amendment Today

For the person who has no money at all, any bail may be considered "excessive." This is now being recognized by many judges and students of the criminal law. A few years ago the Attorney General of the United States called together a national conference on bail and criminal justice. Studies of this matter have been carried on in New York, the District of Columbia, and elsewhere. One procedure being experimented with is to permit accused persons whose backgrounds show them to be "reasonably good risks" to be relieved from custody "on their own recognizance."

National attention is also being directed to the question of whether or not a long delay of execution is not a cruel and unusual punishment in and of itself. In the Chessman case[40] the arguments were made and then turned down that the repeated postponements of the death sentence could be considered cruel and unusual punishment, even though they resulted from legal proceedings started by the condemned man. The same argument may be urged when one whose execution has been put off because of insanity is ordered to be executed after his sanity returns.

Of course, the oldest controversy is whether, by contemporary standards, the death sentence itself might not be cruel and unusual punishment.

By its decision in the Witherspoon case,[41] the Supreme Court has encouraged the drive for the abolition of capital punishment. In sixteenth century England about two hundred and fifty different types of crimes, including petty offenses, were punishable by death. In America today, as a practical matter, the death penalty can be enforced for only three types of crime—murder, kidnapping, and rape. In thirteen states capital punishment has been eliminated completely or can be recommended only in special situations.[42]

According to national polls, in 1966 almost half of the American people were against capital punishment. Yet, a scant fifteen years ago, sixty-eight percent of the population was in favor of the death penalty. Even in those parts of the country where it is still legally permissible, the tide of public opinion has stemmed the number of executions. Only two people were executed in 1967; one was executed in 1966. In 1930 one hundred and ninety-nine persons suffered the death penalty.

To date the Supreme Court has avoided a direct confrontation with the question of whether or not the death penalty should be abolished. Instead, the Court has been gingerly picking away at the fringes.

9. Civil Rights After the Civil War

AMENDMENTS XIII, XIV, XIX and XXIV

PRESIDENT JOHN Quincy Adams once said that the distribution of powers between the federal government and the states had resulted in giving Americans "the most complicated government on the face of the globe." In 1861 this complex system of government was faced with its most serious crisis when eleven states announced that they had the power to leave the federal union. These states then proceeded to secede and set up their own confederacy. It took four years of bloody war, led by our martyred President Abraham Lincoln, to reinstitute the principle of the federal union. Although, ultimately, many southern leaders accepted the military defeat of the Confederacy, they still did not believe that the federal government had a right to override the states in many areas. This controversy over states' rights gradually abated, but it has never ended, and, even in the twentieth century, it has engendered controversy between federal and state officials with respect to a number of problems.

At the end of the Civil War the Thirteenth Amendment was proposed. It was adopted in order to carry out the determination of the northern forces and to fulfill the commitment of Abraham Lincoln to wipe out slavery. The amendment stated:

> Neither slavery nor involuntary servitude except as a punishment for a crime whereof the party shall have been duly convicted, shall exist within the United States, or any place subject to their jurisdiction.

The Thirteenth Amendment was approved by the legislatures of the states with very little opposition. Congress thereafter enacted legislation which sought to make sure that the freed slaves received the same legal protection as white citizens. However, questions about the validity of these laws were raised, and there was a strong demand for another constitutional amendment to clear up the legal controversies.

During the debate over the various proposals which finally culminated in the Fourteenth Amendment, there were many heated arguments. Senator Browning of Illinois was one of the many who foresaw serious consequences:

> If the proposed amendments of the Constitution be adopted, new and enormous power will be claimed and exercised by Congress as warranted by these amendments, and the whole structure of our Government will perhaps gradually yet surely be revolutionized. And so will the Judiciary. If the proposed amendments be adopted, they may and certainly will be used substantially to annihilate the state judiciaries. . . . Be assured that if this new provision be engrafted in the Constitution, it will, in time, change the entire structure and texture of our Government, and sweep away all the guaranties of safety devised and provided by our patriotic sires of the revolution.

As finally adopted, the Fourteenth Amendment was watered down to meet some of these objections. The first section of the Fourteenth Amendment reads in part:

> No State shall make or enforce any law which shall abridge the privileges or immunities of citizens of the United States; nor shall any State deprive any person of life, liberty, or property without due process of law; nor deny to any person within its jurisdiction the equal protection of the laws.

Section 2 continues:

> Representatives shall be apportioned among the several

States according to their respective numbers, counting the whole number of persons in each State, excluding Indians not taxed.

Before the passage of the Fourteenth Amendment the states always had enjoyed almost unrestricted power to make laws affecting the lives, liberties, and properties of their citizens. The Fourteenth Amendment stated that they could not use these powers to "abridge the privileges or immunities of citizens of the United States," nor could they refuse to grant anyone "equal protection of the laws." Even in its modified form this amendment was fought as an assault and an encroachment upon the "sovereign powers" of the states. It was denounced as a betrayal of the principles of the American Revolution. However, this outcry and the resistance subsided somewhat when the states' rights people saw that the Supreme Court was generally inclined to interpret and apply the amendment very cautiously.

The Fifteenth Amendment provided:

The right of citizens of the United States to vote shall not be denied or abridged by the United States or by any State on account of race, color, or previous condition of servitude.

To clear up any question of authority, each one of these three amendments provided that Congress could enforce it "by appropriate legislation." These amendments were all ratified by 1870. The Nineteenth Amendment, in 1919, gave women the right to vote; and, in 1964, the Twenty-Fourth Amendment, abolishing the poll tax which restricted the right to vote, was quickly ratified.

Although the Civil War essentially had been fought over the question of whether the federal union or the states had final power over fundamental issues, the Court was still reluctant to act upon the implications of the victory of the Union forces. For a third of a century, from 1868 to 1897, the Court restricted its role to that of a "balancing body, restoring the balance between the states and the national government while sitting as a judge upon cases."

The justices of the Supreme Court were reluctant to declare laws of state legislatures unconstitutional and, as a matter of fact, did not do so often in the years immediately following the Civil War. However, as the last third of the century drew near, the United States, that farming and agricultural country loved by Jefferson and Madison, began to turn into the huge commercial and industrial complex that Alexander Hamilton had foreseen. This change in the country's economic and business system brought in its wake tremendous changes in the lives of millions of citizens who left the farms and became wage earners in the factories and mills.

The emerging problems put the legislatures of the individual states under pressure to control the property and activities of these new industrial organizations. The railroads and other large business organizations were successful in their attempts to have the Supreme Court invalidate state laws designed to restrict these business operations.

The Fourteenth Amendment read, in part:

> No State shall make or enforce any law which shall abridge the privileges or immunities of citizens of the United States; nor shall any State deprive any person of life, liberty, or property, without due process of law; nor deny to any person within its jurisdiction the equal protection of the laws.

Since a corporation was defined by the Court as a "legal person," it came within the protection of the Fourteenth Amendment, which was said to apply to "any person."

Lawyers and judges pondered, twisted, and debated the meaning of some of the words and phrases in this section for almost one hundred years. The first important case appealed to the Supreme Court involving the Fourteenth Amendment[1] was a lawsuit commenced by an association of New Orleans butchers. They sought to invalidate a statute passed by the Louisiana Legislature which granted a single New Orleans corporation a monopoly on the slaughtering of livestock.

The attorneys for the butchers' association claimed that these butchers had been deprived of some of the "privileges" and "immunities" to which they were entitled as "citizens of the United States," namely, the right to engage in the slaughter house business in New Orleans, with "immunities" from state prosecution. The attorney for the butchers' association argued before the Court that the Fourteenth Amendment had thrown a protective shield around the right to conduct any lawful business.

In its decision the Court rejected this view. Five justices said that the state of Louisiana had a right to determine who might operate the slaughter houses in New Orleans. The "privileges" of citizenship of the United States did not give any butcher an absolute right, under the Constitution, to engage in the slaughter house business. The minority criticized this interpretation of the Fourteenth Amendment by saying it would result in a revolutionary change in the relationship of the nation to the states, and that it would make the Supreme Court the final arbitrator.

In that case the Privileges or Immunities Clause was interpreted by the majority of the Court as covering only certain specific rights, such as the right to travel freely through the United States, equal "right to use the navigable waters of the United States," and a few other elemental rights of that sort. The majority stated that, except for a few qualifications, the "entire domain of privileges and immunities of the citizens of the states . . . lay within the constitutional legislative power of the states, and without that of the Federal Government." They did not believe that the Fourteenth Amendment was designed to "transfer the security and protection of all civil rights . . . from the states to the Federal Government."

As late as the early portion of this century the majority of the Supreme Court adhered to the philosophy that most areas of personal concern should be left to state control. In the last half-century, however, the emergence of problems which are considered national in scope and require vast outlays of capital,

coupled with demands by citizens for new governmental services, has resulted in retraction of some of the powers of state
governments and expansion of those of the federal government.
It seems unlikely that this trend will abate.

It had been hoped by the freed Negro slaves that the adoption
of the Thirteenth, Fourteenth, and Fifteenth Amendments following the bloody Civil War would finally give them all the
rights and liberties of other citizens. However, the southern
states saw the demands of the Negroes as a threat to the superior
position of the white race. These states employed all of their
power to keep the federal government from taking control of
the administration of civil rights and liberties.

The United States Congress, in 1875, passed a series of civil
rights acts intended to give the Negroes full equal status with
other Americans. However, the Supreme Court decided that the
enforcement of the Fourteenth Amendment did not give Congress power to take action against "private persons" accused of
wrongdoings involving the rights of either Negroes or whites.

In a decision in 1883[2] the Court held further that the protection of civil rights was left in the hands of the states, rather than
of the national government. In spite of the language of the
amendment, the Court insisted that the Fourteenth Amendment
had made no essential change in this area of legislation.

There seems to be little doubt that the people who drafted
the Fourteenth Amendment felt it should incorporate the principles and provisions of the Bill of Rights so as to restrict action
by the individual states. However, these views had not been
made loudly and clearly enough for the judges who sat on the
Supreme Court of the United States during the latter portion of
the last century and the first quarter of the twentieth century.

The Fourteenth Amendment said nothing about "separate but
equal" facilities being provided for members of the white and
colored races on railroad trains or in educational institutions.
Yet, the Supreme Court, in 1896, decided that it did not violate
the clause calling for "equal protection of laws" to separate

Negroes from whites in railroad coaches.[3] As long as the accommodations were "substantially equal," the Court felt that fair treatment was being given. The doctrine of "separate but equal" was maintained for more than a half century.

Today, many of the essential elements of the federal Bill of Rights have been encompassed by the Fourteenth Amendment and made applicable to the states. This trend was characterized by Justice Benjamin Cardozo as a "process of absorption." In an opinion handed down in 1937, Cardozo explained, "The process of absorption had its source in the belief that neither liberty nor justice would exist if... [those guaranties] were sacrificed."[4]

In one case[5] the High Court came close to incorporating the entire Bill of Rights into the Fourteenth Amendment. In 1947 a man named Adamson, who had been convicted of murder by a California court, appealed to the Supreme Court. He claimed that he had not received a fair trial and urged that the Due Process of Law Clause of the amendment protected him. The majority of the Court decided that the "due process clause of the Fourteenth Amendment, however, does not draw all of the rights of the Federal Bill of Rights under its protection."

However, a minority of four, speaking through Justice Hugo Black, asserted that the amendment had made all the provisions of the charter of liberties effective in state courts as well as federal. Black stated that his review of the debates leading to passage of the amendment had persuaded him:

> One of the chief objects that the provisions of the Amendment's first section, separately, and as a whole, were intended to accomplish was to make the Bill of Rights applicable to the states ... This historic purpose has never received full consideration or exposition in any opinion of this court interpreting the Amendment. . . .
>
> I fear to see the consequences of the Court's practice of substituting its own concepts of decency and fundamental justice for the language of the Bill of Rights. I would follow what I believe was the original purpose of the Fourteenth Amendment

—to extend to all people of the nation complete protection of the Bill of Rights. To hold that this Court can determine what, if any, provisions of the Bill of Rights will be enforced, and if so, to what degree, is to frustrate the great design of a written Constitution.

In a speech delivered in February, 1961, at the New York University School of Law, Justice William J. Brennan Jr. indicated which of the important safeguards in the federal Bill of Rights he believed were to be applied to the states.

He enumerated the protection for religion, press, assembly, and petition; the requirement that "just compensation" shall be paid for private property taken for public use; the right to counsel in criminal cases; and the guarantees against unreasonable searches and seizures. He stated:

> It is reason for deep satisfaction that many of the states effectively enforce the counterparts in state constitutions of the specifics of the Bill of Rights. Indeed, some have been applied by the states to an extent beyond that required of the national government by the corresponding federal guaranty. But too many state practices fall far short. Far too many cases come from the states to the Supreme Court presenting dismal pictures of official lawlessness, of illegal searches and seizures, illegal detentions attended by prolonged interrogation and coerced admissions of guilt, of the denial of counsel, and downright brutality. Judicial self-restraint, which defers too much to the sovereign powers of the states and reserves judicial intervention for only the most revolting cases, will not serve to enhance Madison's priceless gift of "the great rights of mankind secured under this Constitution." For these secure the only climate in which the law of freedom can exist.

In recent decades the Court has invoked the Fourteenth Amendment to halt or restrain many state activities. The amendment has been used to outlaw state laws forbidding peaceful picketing; to invalidate laws compelling organizers for unions to register with state agencies; to set aside state court contempt proceedings against persons who were accused of using the press to influence court decisions; to void state sedition laws on the grounds that Congress had passed its own legislation covering the same field. The Supreme Court has detailed standards for the states to follow in the areas of administration of the criminal law and trials. The Court also has been most zealous in recent years in affirming the constitutional guaranties afforded to Negroes in their struggle for equality and in assuring a fair apportionment of the state legislators.

POLITICAL FREEDOM

In this century the most significant impact of the Supreme Court on civil rights under the Constitution has been on the rights of the Negro.

The Right to Vote

With the monumental decision of the High Court in *Smith* v. *Allwright*[6] the political history of the South and, hence, of the nation was changed forever. That case and the ones that followed during the next decade underscored the principle that freedom to vote, without discrimination could not be vitiated, either directly or indirectly, by the states, no matter how subtle or sophisticated was the state machinery for disenfranchisement. In the *Smith* v. *Allwright* case the white primary was outlawed in both state and local elections. The state was not permitted to veil its unconstitutional purpose by hiding behind the form of a private organization or by any procedure through which a private group could deprive the Negro of the right to vote because of his race.

Other techniques for preventing the Negro from voting, such as grandfather clauses and restricted registration requirements have also been ruled by the Supreme Court to be violations of the Fourteenth and Fifteenth Amendments. Actually, as a legal matter, the cases relating to suffrage have left no conceivable legal basis upon which Negroes may be disenfranchised because of color.

In 1964 the Constitution was augmented by the Twenty-Fourth Amendment which outlawed the poll tax in national elections. The first time the Supreme Court was faced with an interpretation of this amendment was in 1965 when it invalidated an attempt by the Virginia legislature to get around the poll tax by requiring prospective voters to file formal certificates of residence at least six months before the election unless they paid the same poll tax imposed for state elections.

In addition, the poll tax has now also been outlawed in state elections. Since it was, in essence, a method of discriminating between poor and rich it was held to violate the "equal protection laws" as required by the Fourteenth Amendment.[7]

Legislative Apportionment

The doctrine of "equal protection of laws" under the Fourteenth Amendment and the idea that the states could not, either directly or indirectly, use their authority to restrict primaries to white people was applied to another deterrent to effective suffrage. For a long time it had been argued that the county-unit system and the malapportionment of state legislatures had watered down the importance of the vote of certain segments of the population, principally that of urban and suburban residents, as compared with that of people living in rural areas of the states. While the county-unit systems of Georgia, Maryland, and Mississippi did not actually deprive citizens of the vote, they did dilute the importance of some people's votes, making them more or less powerless in selecting representatives to be sent to the legislatures. In addition, many districts were "gerrymandered"—i.e., the district lines were drawn so as to favor those already in power—thus further debasing the votes of

Negroes in the South and of urban dwellers elsewhere.

The landmark case of *Baker* v. *Carr*[8] clarified the jurisdiction of the federal courts in cases of legislative malapportionment. This case involved a suit initiated in the federal District Court of Tennessee under the Civil Rights Acts of 1875 to correct claimed violations of constitutional rights. The claim was that a 1901 Tennessee statute arbitrarily apportioned the seats of the general assembly among the ninety-five counties of the state. Since there had been substantial growth and redistribution of Tennessee's population, failure to reapportion the seats was held to debase many people's votes and, thus, to deny them the equal protection of laws assured by the Fourteenth Amendment. The District Court dismissed the complaint, deciding that it lacked jurisdiction in this type of dispute and, therefore, that it could not grant relief. However, the Supreme Court reversed this decision, writing that the "right asserted is within the judicial reach of the judicial protection under the Fourteenth Amendment."

In *Reynolds* v. *Sims*[9] the Court set forth the tests to be used in deciding the appropriateness of the apportionment of a state legislature. On June 14, 1964, the Court invalidated the apportionment of legislative seats in Alabama, Colorado, Delaware, Maryland, New York, and Virginia. The Court's decision was based on the belief that the existing allocation of seats violated the provision of the Fourteenth Amendment guaranteeing the equal protection of laws.

In reaching its conclusion, the Court started from the premise that the inequality of representation was not simply a political matter, but that the rights denied also were highly personal in nature—that it was the individual right of the qualified voter to have an effective say in the conduct of government. If the vote of an individual in one district was less effective than the vote of an individual in another district within the same state, this was a contradiction of the constitutional basis of the right to vote. The Court, therefore, concluded that the state laws do not give equal protection unless the seats in the two houses of a bicameral legislature are apportioned on the basis of population. Voting should be based on the standard of one man—one vote. "The weight of a citizen's vote cannot be made to depend on where he lives."

The concept of one-man, one-vote was further extended by the Supreme Court to city, town, and county legislative bodies in *Avery* v. *Midland County*.[10] That case involved a commissioner's court made up of four men, each elected from four separate districts. However, the representative from the major portion of the city of Midland had many more constituents than the three rural members all had together. Mayor Hank Avery of Midland sued. The majority, by a five to three vote, did not hesitate to take action with respect to the over-representation of the rural areas. The Court ruled that this method of selecting representatives was unfair because the commission was the general governing body of the entire county. It implied that it might have decided differently if the case concerned "a special-purpose unit of government assigned the performance of functions affecting definable groups of constituents"—functions such as building roads or setting up schools. It has been estimated that twenty-thousand local units of government will be affected by this case.

DISCRIMINATION AND EQUAL PROTECTION OF LAW

The thrust of the Supreme Court into the political thicket of voting and apportionment of legislative seats has been matched by its involvement in problems of racial discrimination in social activities such as the ownership and occupancy of residential real estate, the use of facilities of public transportation, the availability of educational opportunities, and the enjoyment of places of public accommodation.

Residential Property

Since 1948 the Supreme Court has gone a long way to insure Negroes the legal right to the ownership and occupancy of real estate.[11] The present view of the Court is that the states cannot use their legal authority to participate in such discrimination. For a substantial period of time the Supreme Court had adhered to the position that the Fourteenth Amendment prevents private property owners from agreeing with each other through restrictive covenants not to rent or sell their property to Negroes.[12] For many years these covenants were regarded as private, rather than state, action; and, therefore, they were not believed to fall within the reach of the Fourteenth Amendment. However, in 1948, the Supreme Court decided that, when state courts enforced racially restrictive covenants, this was *state* action which deprived Negroes of the equal protection of laws guaranteed them under the Fourteenth Amendment.[13]

Nevertheless, there remained some open questions. In 1950 the Supreme Court refused to review the New York Court of Appeals' decision that a private housing corporation could keep Negroes out of a housing project even though the project had been constructed through the state's power of eminent domain and enjoyed a twenty-five year New York City tax exemption.[14] In another case in which the state court had refused to strike down discrimination stemming from a private agreement, the Supreme Court held that this action was not a violation of the Fourteenth Amendment.[15]

Many decisions by the Supreme Court, three constitutional amendments, and more than half a dozen federal laws have not been enough to exorcise the ghost of prejudice in America. A bitterly fought Civil Rights Law of 1968 seemed to be an important legal step in eliminating racially segregated housing, but a much more important step in the direction of freedom from discrimination has been the 1968 decision of the Supreme Court in the Jones case.[16] The Court's clearly stated intention in this case was to end "*all* racial discrimination, private as well as public, in the sale or rental of property." It seems to make the Civil Rights Act of 1968 virtually unnecessary.

In 1965 Mr. and Mrs. Joseph Lee Jones tried to purchase a $30,000 home in a St. Louis development. They brought suit against the developer when they were turned down because Mr. Jones was a Negro. In writing his brief, their lawyer threw in an 1866 federal statute as a makeweight argument. The Supreme Court justified its decision in the case mainly on the basis of this statute.

The statute of 1866 expresses unequivocally that all "citizens of the United States shall have the same right, in every state and territory, as is enjoyed by white citizens thereof, to inherit, purchase, lease, sell, hold and convey real and personal property." In the Jones case Justice Potter Stewart pointed out that Congress had not made a distinction between private and state discrimination even though it had had the power to do so under the Thirteenth Amendment. Justice Stewart went on to say, "So long as a Negro citizen who wants to buy or rent a home can be turned away simply because he is not white, he cannot be said to enjoy 'the same right as is enjoyed by white citizens.' "

The majority was convinced by its study of the legislative history of the Civil Rights Act of 1866 that the congressmen of that day had understood the broad sweep of its language.

John Harlan, however, disagreed with such a reading and dissented from the majority's opinion. He stated:

> The individualistic ethic of their time emphasized personal freedom and embodied a distaste for governmental interference. It seems to me that more of these men would have regarded it as a great intrusion on individual liberty for the government to take from a man the power to refuse for personal reasons to enter into a purely private transaction.

He also pointed out that in 1968, just before the decision of the Court in the Jones case, Congress had exempted from its restrictions those individuals who sell their own property without using a real estate agent or who rent rooms in a boarding house that they own and live in. The majority countered this argument with the assertion that the Civil Rights Act of 1968 expressly stated that it did not supersede any prior civil rights statute. They also said that, since the 1968 ruling calls for punishment of those who discriminate, it is different from the 1866 Act which did not prescribe any penalties.

Other Negroes may find it difficult to prove discrimination in housing if they try to force their right in a law suit. The 1866 Statute, according to Stewart, gave assurance that Negroes have "the freedom to buy whatever a white man can buy, to live wherever a white man can live." Stewart stated that, "if Congress cannot say that being a free man means at least this much," then freeing the slaves was "a promise that the nation cannot keep."

In addition to the Jones case's impact on housing, a footnote to Justice Potter Stewart's opinion appears to give new stability to another 1866 law. This statute promised all persons an equal right to "make and enforce contracts." Some lawyers have advanced the idea that the 1866 contract law could become a more comprehensive "fair employment" statute than the present one, which does not cover all employees. Other areas of application might be insurance, financing, brokerage, and personal service contracts such as those of doctors, dentists, barbers, and others who may perhaps discriminate. While most racial discrimination cases have been tried under the guarantee of the "equal protections of the laws," this case may bring about the use of the Thirteenth Amendment to end all vestiges of slavery.

Transportation Facilities

The cases dealing with public transportation facilities have followed a twisted course for more than half a century. They have relied for legal principle on two constitutional provisions: Article I, Section 8, which gives Congress the authority to regulate interstate commerce, and the portion of the Fourteenth Amendment that requires equal protection of the laws.

The law was dominated for a long time by the case of *Plessy* v. *Ferguson*[17], which was decided in 1896. A Louisiana statute required separate and equal accommodations for white and colored persons on railroads in that state. In the Plessy v. Ferguson case this was held to be a valid exercise of the power of the state to preserve peace and order, rather than an invalid deprivation of the equal protection of the laws. Justice Henry Billings Brown justified this decision, to a large extent, on his view that the position of the Negro plaintiff was predicated on "the assumption that the enforced separation of the two races stamps the colored race with a badge of inferiority," and Justice Brown added that, "If this be so, it is not by reason of anything found in the act, but solely because the colored race chooses to put that construction upon it."

One of the commentators on this case has written, "The opinion of the Court in *Plessy* v. *Ferguson* is a compound of bad logic, bad history, bad sociology, and bad constitutional law."[18]

The concept of "separate but equal" was applied henceforth to perpetrate what was actually an inequality of treatment between the races. While the state principle of constitutional dogma was "separate but equal," the Supreme Court was most reluctant, until a quarter of a century ago, to insist upon facilities which were, in fact, equal. This was especially true with respect to educational facilities.

Until 1941 the Commerce Clause was not applied very much more effectively by the courts in breaking down segregated transportation. In *Mitchell* v. *United States*[19] a Negro congressman traveled on a train ticket which entitled him to Pullman accommodations. When the train went into Arkansas, he was required to ride in the day coach provided for Negroes, rather than in the Pullman car. The railroad ostensibly afforded col-

ored passengers equal but separate facilities in accordance with
the Arkansas act permitting Negroes desiring Pullman accommodations to buy drawing room space at usual Pullman rates.
This time, however, there were no drawing rooms available, and
Congressman Mitchell complained to the Interstate Commerce
Commission, which dismissed his grievance. The Supreme Court
decided in his favor under the federal statute forbidding racial
discrimination by railroads. The test of equality had not been
satisfied.

In 1946, in *Morgan* v. *Virginia*,[20] the Supreme Court invalidated a Virginia statute calling for segregation on interstate, as
well as intrastate, buses. The case concerned the prosecution of
a Negro woman who would not move to the rear of a bus going
from Virginia to Baltimore, Maryland, although the driver had
requested her to move. The Court held that the segregation law
was a burden on interstate commerce in matters where uniform-
ity was required, and this decision was used as a guide in a
number of succeeding cases.[21] It is noteworthy that, while the
Supreme Court insisted on a factual equality in these later transportation cases, it never rejected the concept of "separate but
equal." The attack against this doctrine was saved for the field
of education.

Education

In the field of education, from the time of the Plessy decision
until 1954, the Supreme Court concentrated its attack against
racial segregation on the inequality of the separate facilities.
Segregation itself was not directly challenged for a long time.
In 1938, in the case of *Missouri ex rel Gaines* v. *Canada*,[22] it was
decided that Missouri had deprived a Negro of equal protection
of the laws when he was not admitted to the University of Missouri Law School but, instead, was offered his tuition fees for
a law school in a state which did not segregate. In this case the

Court actually looked into the question of whether the state afforded *de facto* equality of facilities. The Court also made this investigation in the case of *Sweatt* v. *Painter*,[23] in which it was decided that the Texas law school for Negroes did not actually measure up to the University of Texas Law School. And, in another case, the Court also held that, if a Negro had been admitted to a state university by order of a court, segregation of his activities prevented him from full opportunity to follow his field of graduate work and, hence, was a denial of equal protection.[24]

In 1954 the High Court considered a number of cases dealing with the racial segregation of children in the public schools of South Carolina, Virginia, Delaware, and Kansas. In the epochal decision of *Brown* v. *Board of Education*,[25] Chief Justice Earl Warren, speaking for the Court, concluded that the concept of "separate but equal" was an improper approach to public education and that the plaintiffs "had been deprived of the equal protection of the laws guaranteed by the Fourteenth Amendment" since "separate educational facilities are inherently unequal."

A year later the Supreme Court announced, "implementation of these constitutional principles may require the solution of varied local school problems."[26] In this case the Court went on to say that the factors which could be considered included such elements as:

> the physical condition of the school plant, the school transportation system, personnel, revision of school districts and attendance areas into compact units to achieve a system of determining admission to the public schools on a nonracial basis, and revision of local laws and regulations which may be necessary in solving the foregoing problems.

The Court ruled that the "primary responsibility for elucidating, assessing, and solving these problems" should fall on the local school boards. The federal district courts were assigned the obligation of deciding "whether the action of the school authorities constitutes good faith implementation of the governing constitutional principles." These courts were directed to see that the school officials "make a prompt and reasonable start toward full compliance" and proceed toward desegregation "with all deliberate speed."

The past decade has seen much resistance to attempts to desegregate public schools, and there has been only desultory success. The federal district courts have had to face all sorts of dilatory procedural tactics. In a number of states the legislatures have passed resolutions invoking the long interred doctrine of "interposition"—i.e., the doctrine that a state government can render an act of Congress inoperable within that state by interposing its authority between the act and the people of the state. The states have also tried to avoid integration by passing laws closing public schools, providing for the special transfer of pupils, depriving integrated schools of state funds, ending compulsory school attendance, providing tuition grants to "private" schools, and allowing free choice of schools. Persons and organizations seeking to carry out the mandate of the Supreme Court have been hampered and harassed. Nevertheless, it does not seem likely that anyone will actually be able to stop the movement toward desegregation of the schools.

This was recently underscored by the Supreme Court of the United States.[27] Writing for an exasperated and unanimous court, Justice William Brennan wrote, "The burden on a school board today is to come forward with a plan that promises realistically to work, and promises realistically to work *now*."

He uttered the Court's displeasure with the "freedom of choice" schemes that over thirteen hundred school districts in the South have used. In the two counties specifically studied by the Court, it was found that segregation persisted, largely because the onus of requesting school transfers had been left to the Negro pupils. The Court stated that it was the local school boards, rather than the Negro pupils, who were "clearly charged with the affirmative duty to take whatever steps might be necessary to convert to a unitary system in which racial discrimination would be eliminated root and branch."

Many of those interested in this field of civil rights saw in this ruling a "get tough" attitude that sought concrete results in the northern de facto segregated schools, as well as in the South.

Private Facilities Open to the Public

In the civil rights cases[28] of 1883 the Supreme Court decided that places of public accommodation, such as hotels, restaurants, and private transportation facilities, could practice discrimination without violating the Fourteenth Amendment because their acts were private, rather than those of the state. Today, the line between private and public action is becoming more difficult to draw and, in dealing with racial problems, the courts have ruled against discrimination, even in what might otherwise be regarded as private acts.

It is possible to see this breakdown of the line between public and private action when we examine several cases chronologically. Thus, in 1961, the High Court decided that a restaurant operated privately but leased from a municipality could not refuse to serve Negroes. In 1963, in five cases involving sit-ins at privately owned lunch counters, the Court held that the cities in which the stores were located had violated the equal protection of the laws under the Fourteenth Amendment. The rationale of the opinion was that the muncipalities were parties to the discrimination because they had made racial segregation a policy of state, either through ordinance or public expression by the officials concerned.[30] A year later, in *Griffin* v. *Maryland*,[31] the Court found that there had been a violation of the Fourteenth Amendment because a private police officer who caused an arrest based on racial discrimination had been made a deputy sheriff. In *Robinson* v. *Florida*,[32] decided the same year, the Supreme Court reversed the conviction for trespass of sit-in demonstrators at a restaurant on the grounds that the department of health's requirement that restaurants provide separate toilet facilities for each race "whether employed or served in the restaurant," was a state action.

Congress took the next step that same year when it prohibited discrimination in places of public accommodation, even if they were privately owned. And on December 14, 1964, the Supreme Court upheld the Civil Rights Act of 1964's provisions relating to facilities for public accommodations. In one case[33] a motel serving interstate travelers sought to stop the enforcement of Title II of the Civil Rights Act of 1964. This motel had refused to offer its facilities to Negroes because of their race and took the position that it would continue to do so unless the Civil Rights Act as applied to it was ruled constitutional. The Supreme Court based its decision on the commerce clause, rather than the Equal Protection Clause. The Court found "overwhelming evidence that discrimination by hotels and motels impedes interstate travel [and] had the effect of discouraging travel on the part of substantial portions of the Negro community."

In an accompanying case[34] the Court found that Congress had more than a sufficient basis to decide that racial discrimination at restaurants, which derived a substantial portion of the food they served from other states, had a direct and inhibiting effect on interstate commerce.

10. Civil Rights and the Constitution in the Sixth Decade

It must be apparent, even to a casual observer of the American scene, that the final arbiter, and certainly a major innovator, of public policy during the past quarter of a century has been the Supreme Court of the United States. Without expressing a value judgment, it must be pointed out that this assertion of authority by the Court, principally in the field of civil rights, has resulted in a number of political problems which remain to be resolved.

THE BASIS FOR JUDICIAL INTERVENTION

It has been noted that no place in the Constitution is the Supreme Court given express power to exercise what has traditionally been regarded as legislative authority—the authority to promulgate broad principles of public policy to be acted upon in the future. The Constitution, in Article III, Section 2, provides only that "judicial power shall extend to all cases, in law and equity, arising under this Constitution, the laws of the United States, and treaties made, or which shall be made, under their authority." As a matter of fact, in Article I, legislative powers are vested "in a Congress of the United States, which shall consist of a Senate and House of Representatives."

The Supreme Court has justified its exercise of power on the basis of two concepts which have not been successfully challenged. The first is the doctrine of "judicial review—the idea that a statute can be tested against the requirements of the Constitution and then voided if, in the opinion of the Court, it does not meet the challenge. The second basis for the Supreme Court's power is its belief in its right to interpret the Fourteenth Amendment, which provides:

> No State shall make or enforce any law which shall abridge the privileges or immunities of citizens of the United States; nor shall any State deprive any person of life, liberty, or property, without due process of law; nor deny to any person within its jurisdiction the equal protection of the laws.

As has been shown,[1] the implications of the Equal Protection of the Laws Clause were not realized for a long time. This clause was applied by the Court narrowly at first on the theory that it was simply designed to insure the end of slavery, rather than to relate to any state action affecting living persons or corporations.

In the course of the hundred years which followed the Civil War, the essential character of American life was transformed. The frontier became an agrarian society which then became an urban one, dependent upon an interlocking system of industrial and financial interests. Control over these aggregations of power has now passed from individuals to a relatively few monolithic organizations, the major corporations and unions. To a large extent the federal government has assumed the obligation of maintaining the health and vitality of the economic system.

In part, the effort to keep this vast business system running on an even keel has generated enormous pressure on consumer demand for goods and services. Newer products are constantly being invented. Newer health care techniques are being discovered. Newer uses of leisure time are being developed. As a result of this pressure, coupled with higher real wages and more leisure time brought about by automation and other industrial techniques, the level of expectation of the ordinary citizen continues to rise. While there are still serious pockets of poverty and discrimination in America, to a very substantial degree what were formerly considered the advantages of the idle rich have now become necessities for the masses. And the community, by a concern for the ill, aged, and impoverished, may perhaps be accused of promoting the "survival of the unfittest." People have ultimately turned to the national, state, and local governments to satisfy the new expectations and demands.

In addition, the technological advances made necessary by the automtaion of the economy, the exploitation of nuclear forces, the drive to explore space, and the frantic pace of experimentation in the overlap of biology-chemistry-physics place an insuperable financial burden on the private sector, resourceful as the efforts to pool private capital may be. For this reason, among others, the staggering outlay of capital and expenditure of funds for these vast undertakings have been accomplished, for the most part, by government.

THE CHANGING CONCEPT OF "EQUAL PROTECTION"

In this context what is the significance of the promise of the Fourteenth Amendment that no state shall "deny to any person within its jurisdiction the equal protection of the laws"? When adopted after the Civil War, this provision was construed simply as forbidding a state from actually discriminating against "any person within its jurisdiction" by some act.[2] Later, the Court went on to rule that, if a state did not take steps to remove a discriminating condition, it was violating "the equal protection of the laws."[3] Finally, the Court took another significant step and ruled that, if the state did not do everything in its power to assure "equal protection of the laws" with respect to a given area of discrimination, the federal courts would themselves enunciate the directives which the state legislature had failed or refused to enact and would attempt to implement them by court decree.[4]

THE REVOLUTION IN AMERICAN SOCIETY

Some time ago Justice Abe Fortas stated in a lecture, "It is fascinating, although disconcerting to some, that the first and fundamental breakthrough in various categories of *revolutionary progress* has been made by the courts and specifically, the Supreme Court of the United States."[5] And in a penetrating analysis of the role of the Court, Adolf Berle has written:

> Use of the word "revolution" implies no criticism of the Court. I think it could not have acted otherwise than it did. Far from arrogating to itself powers it did not have, the Court's latent constitutional powers granted it by the Fourteenth Amendment were activated by the pace of technical and social change. When this history is written, it will probably be found that the Supreme Court's action saved the country from a far more dangerous and disorderly change.

Education

It has been pointed out that, in *Brown* v. *Board of Education*[7] the Supreme Court used the "equal protection of laws" in the Fourteenth Amendment to prohibit the segregation of Negro children in state-supported public schools. But the Court did more than strike down state action. By authorizing the lower federal courts to issue decrees correcting the inequitable state of affairs in public schools, it, in effect, gave permission to these courts to take affirmative steps to insure the equal protection of the laws.

The Supreme Court gave this permission explicitly in *Bell* v. *Maryland*[8] when it recognized that the lower courts should not only *prohibit* segregation in the public schools, they should also set about to *establish* public schools without segregation. Thus, in this case, the Court went beyond the invocation of the traditional negative judicial remedy—an injunction forbidding certain conduct. It created a new public policly and, then, directed the various local district courts to implement what was essentially legislative action.

Suffrage and Apportionment

In *Baker* v. *Carr*[9] an action was commenced in the Tennessee federal court. A group of citizens argued that their votes did not carry as much weight as other votes in the state and that, as citizens, they were, thus, being denied the equal protection of the laws. They asked the court to rule that the current mode of apportionment in Tennessee was invalid, that further elections be stayed until this system was changed, and, in addition, that the district court should establish a new system of apportionment. The Supreme Court granted the first two demands. It vacated Tennessee's method of apportionment, and it espoused the principle of one man—one vote. However, instead of establishing a new system of apportionment, it sent the matter back to the lower court for appropriate action there, without specifying the precise solution. Surprisingly enough, in that state and in others, the courts dealing with problems usually treated by legislatures have generally attained acceptable remedies.

In the 1967–1968 term of the Supreme Court, the justices used the Equal Protection Clause of the Fourteenth Amendment to extend one-man, one-vote so that it applied to city, town, and county legislatures, as well as to state legislatures.[10] Criticizing the voting districts of Midland County, Texas, Justice White spoke for the majority when he said:

The equal-protection clause reaches the exercise of state power however manifested, whether exercised directly or through municipal subdivisions of the state. If the voters residing in oversized districts are denied their constitutional right to participate in the election of State legislators, precisely the same kind of deprivation occurs when the members of a city council, school board, or county governing board are elected from districts of substantially unequal population.

Private Power and State Discrimination

The assertion of supervision by the federal courts via the "equal protection of the laws" provision of the Fourteenth Amendment has by no means been limited to the reorganization of the state legislatures and the local public school systems.

The power of private groups to throttle individual freedom in a way more direct and potent than that of the state has traditionally been outside the grasp of the Constitution. The Bill of Rights prohibits government from invading the individual's freedom to speak out. It does not permit government hiring policies which discriminate on the basis of color or religious creed. It strikes down any attempt by a state to arbitrarily fix conditions of work, such as wages and laws. It forbids efforts by a state agency to deny or take away the right of an individual to carry on his occupation or profession. Yet, consider the power, unchecked by any constitutional guarantee, which private aggregates of power are able to exact over these vital concerns and many others. Consider the restrictive impact on the free dissemination of information wielded by such mass media as the newspaper, the radio, and television. Consider the broad area of discretion which employers have—to hire or fire. Consider the overwhelming power of labor unions to dictate the terms on which a person may work or enter a field of employment. Consider the degree to which "gentlemens' agreements" or "blacklists" maintained by theatrical agencies can determine, the professional fate of performers and artists. Consider the coercive pressure which religious groups can exert to suppress what some may consider to be works of art or literature.

It has been established by authoritative studies that a few hundred corporate Goliaths control the economic life and, to a great extent, mold the scientific, educational, and social life of America, as well as the minds and beliefs of Americans. Not only do these aggregations of corporate power frequently conduct their affairs and negotiations as if they were national entities, rather than mere companies, but, in fact, in many critical areas, they are virtually sovereign. Nor does it seem likely that this trend will change. Quite to the contrary.

While there has been restriction of the arteries of economic mobility for the enterprising worker aspiring to establish his own business, the picture has not been entirely negative. Today, this worker enjoys a real income, a financial security, and an assurance of health care and retirement opportunities unprecedented in history. While he cannot realistically expect to open his own automobile factory or newspaper or bank, he can reasonably expect to be afforded educational opportunities, chances to develop himself as a person, and a standard of living which would have seemed incredible even to his grandfather. At the same time, he is the almost hapless vassal of economic, cultural, and technological forces which he can only dimly perceive. He is in many ways a creature of such organizations as the General Motors Corporation, the American Medical Association, and the Congress of Industrial Organizations.

Does the Constitution have any relevance in shielding the civil rights of the individual from invasion by private associations, as it does with respect to the assertion of the power of government? Under the Fifth and Fourteenth Amendments neither the federal government nor the states may deprive an individual of "life, liberty, or property, without due process of law." And, under the latter amendment, in addition, no state or other local unit of government may "deny to any person within its jurisdiction the equal protection of the laws."

It has been shown that the Supreme Court is willing to intervene when discrimination in legislative apportionment or public school facilities has resulted from "state action." It has directed its attention to private transactions enforced by state action. As we have seen, in *Shelly* v. *Kraemer*[11] a state court was reversed when it used its judicial power to enforce a restrictive covenant among private property owners who had agreed not to sell residential property to Negroes. And, finally, the Supreme Court has moved in to invoke the Constitution where the government has not been acting overtly but merely acquiescing in discriminatory conduct by private individuals or corporations. This is illustrated by the case in which a railroad and a union which had entered into an agreement having the effect of discriminating against Negroes. The High Court ruled that, under the state law, the union had to conform to a standard of non-discriminatory conduct or the statute authorizing the union to represent the worker could be held unconstitutional.[12] What seems obvious is that the distinction between state action and state passivity in the face of private discriminatory conduct is becoming more and more attenuated.

Just as it grows increasingly difficult to draw the line between state action and state inaction, so the interrelation between state action and private action becomes more and more difficult to untwine. It must be borne in mind that freedom of private groups, of private individuals, is a cardinal desideratum of the Bill of Rights, even if the action or opinion of a particular group at a particular time may seem obnoxious to the majority making up the community. Yet, many private groups do not limit themselves to education, persuasion, or exhortation to bring about the acceptance of their special folkways or mores. They may resort to economic pressures, such as boycotts and other actions which might be labeled unconstitutional if indulged in by governmental authorities. It is not always easy to decide whether the freedom *of* the private group or the freedom *from* the private group is more precious in the hierarchy of democratic values.

Another set of vexatious questions arises from the activities and organizations of special interest membership groups such as, for example, an electrical union local or a local medical society. About a decade ago the *Yale Law Journal* made an exhaustive analysis of the American Medical Association in which it was demonstrated that the organization exercised virtually a life-or-death control over the professional lives of the nation's medical personnel.[13] In some jurisdictions, laws seeking to regulate the policies and practices of the local organized medical fraternity have been enacted. This raises the question of whether the conduct of such organizations should not be measured by the yardstick of the Constitution, rather than regulated by new state legislation. It is not an easy question to answer.

Consider the refusal of a bank to grant credit to an individual on some irrational basis now that money seems to be going out of style? Or what about the hypothetical situation in which a car dealer refuses to sell a car on time to a person whose credit rating has been impaired by an incorrect entry in records maintained by a central credit agency? How about the refusal of a pension plan or health care plan to admit an employee because of his age? Unquestionably, better illustrations may be found. But the underlying fact is that the work-a-day world in what has been regarded as the private sector is tended by electronic devices and automated machines which are capable of destroying human freedom and lives as arbitrarily as any agency of government ever has. On the basis of our discussion of legal precedent, it seems arguable that decisions and regulations of corporations and other associations may be reviewed by the courts under the Fourteenth Amendment, since these organizations are all creatures of the State. The unanswered questions are whether the Court ought to extend the constitutional requirements of "due process" and "equal protection of the laws" to such associations and, if so, to what extent this can be done without destroying the quality of freedom for all of us.

THE CONSTITUTIONAL DILEMMA

In order to decide whether a court can interfere with corporate or organizational activity, it must be determined whether an action is "state action," justifying judicial intervention, or private. However, the answer to this question is dependent on the answers to several others. The court must ask to what extent the private activities are inconsistent with public policies adopted by the duly constituted governmental agencies; how serious the threat to constitutional freedoms posed by the private activities is; and to what extent the courts can effectively deal with such problems without engendering new and more difficult ones.

Certainly, the burden of decision should be on those who urged judicial intervention into private action. Moreover, the purpose of the intervention should not be simple vindication of a right—in order for intervention to be justified it must be able to provide a viable remedy within the judicial range. Before the Court acts, should there not be at least substantial evidence that accepted policies on important freedoms are threatened? And, finally, should there not be some assurance that Court action can be effective in solving the problem?

Sharing the Task

The increasingly active role of the Supreme Court has come about because the majority of the justices feel that the legislative branch has not been able to cope with the basic problems of our time. Yet, even the most staunch supporters of a strong Court concede that this growing trend toward judicial intervention has created problems for the federal government "which must be solved if the Supreme Court is not to endanger or lose its mandate through tides of political action."[14]

There has been substantial criticism of the Supreme Court because of the initiative it has shown in the past decade. Thirty-four states have called for a constitutional convention to take away the power of the Supreme Court to deal with "political" matters such as apportionment. Even Justice Hugo Black, who in the past, had always been regarded as a leading judicial activist recently seems to be making a discreet retreat. He says that the labels had been misapplied and, indeed, reversed, and he now complains that the "restraint" position gives "unlimited power" to the judges to invalidate laws they don't like.

Because of this view, he said he could not vote to invalidate, for example, the Connecticut birth control statute, since he found no general rights, implicit in the Bill of Rights. He argued that his position, based strictly on the words and history of the Bill of Rights, carefully limited the power of the judiciary, and, because of this, he criticized the Court for nullifying the Connecticut statute. "Well," he said, "they found some penumbras and emanations from various parts of the Bill of Rights to make a right of privacy. I don't know about penumbras or emanations."[15] This does not sound like the old Hugo L. Black.

At present, the Court lacks a test by which it can accurately determine whether or not intervention is justified. Furthermore, once the Court does decide to intervene and remedy a situation by decree, there are almost insuperable problems of administration and implementation—problems which no court is in a position to solve. In the final analysis, what is, in effect, judicial legislation perhaps should be reserved for emergencies, leaving such action for the most part to the legislative and executive branches, which are more responsive to popular will.

The Warren Court—In Retrospect

Before long Earl Warren, the fourteenth Chief Justice, will become part of American history. But the Warren court will have made an indelible mark on the future life of America. For a decade and a half this Court, which spanned the administrations of Eisenhower, Kennedy, and Johnson, has affected all Americans; and its decisions will continue to do so.

Earlier Chief Justices and their Courts have been dominated by such prevailing interests as property, the adjustment of conflicts between the national government and the states, and slavery. The main theme to which the Warren Court devoted its energies was that of individual rights. By any reckoning of critic and admirer alike the last fifteen years have been the most significant in judicial history since the Court of John Marshall, which established the Supreme Court as the final arbiter of the federal system and almost singlehandedly created a strong national government.

Through the years of Earl Warren's tenure, the Court was subjected to both exuberant praise and vitriolic criticism. After the Supreme Court delivered its prayer rulings, Congressman George Andrews complained, "They put the Negroes in the schools, and now they have driven God out." Senator Everett Dirksen almost got Congress to pass amendments which would have emasculated the prayer and apportionment rulings. The Chief Justices of thirty-six state Supreme Courts approved a resolution criticizing what they deemed the invasion of states' rights by the Supreme Court.

The activism of the Warren Court has been criticized by those who believe in judicial restraint, who feel that the obligation of the Court lies in interpreting the law rather than " in promoting reform when other branches of government fail to act." This is the view of Justice John Harlan. Some legal scholars also charge the Warren court with careless legal craftsmanship in a number of decisions asserting that they complicate rather than elucidate. They claim that many of the major decisions of the court have not been founded on the broad and deep roots of legal precedent, not buttressed by a coherent philosophy of outstanding legal scholarship.

If there could be said to be a single golden thread tying all the rulings of the last fifteen years together, it would be the conviction that the Supreme Court had the responsibility for acting when the other branches of government had not moved to correct basic inequities in the American democracy. This concept was exemplified by the Chief Justices' opinion in *Brown* v. *Board of Education*,[16] decided on May 17, 1965, in which a unanimous Court held segregation in the public schools to be unconstitutional. Wrote Warren, "In the field of public education the doctrine of 'separate but equal' has no place. Separate educational facilities are inherently unequal."

This drive to break down racial barriers continued to the last day of the 1967–1968 term, when the Warren Court outlawed discrimination in the sale and rental of all housing so as to eliminate "the badges of slavery." Among the important decisions that will continue to shape the life of America and its people are those explaining and implementing school desegregation; upholding the validity of the Federal Lobbying Act; safeguarding witnesses appearing before legislative investigating committees; curtailing the irresponsible enforcement of state sedition laws; protecting persons accused of criminal acts; and asserting the fact that fair legislative apportionment is central to a federal system.

Earl Warren has worn the robe of Chief Justice during a period when the beliefs and conditions prevalent throughout the United States were in a state of change. What the times called for was a thoroughgoing reconsideration of the assumed premises of the American society—especially in the area of civil rights and responsibilities. Chief Justice Warren did not shrink from that task.

The comprehensive Crime Control Bill which was signed into law by President Johnson after he had the Chief Justice's letter of resignation in his hand was actually directed against Earl Warren. Its Title II is designed to vitiate the Miranda case and the other decisions which were made to protect accused persons from arbitrary law enforcement. At the present time however, the innovations of the Warren Court seem secure, and its spirit intact.

Prognosis

The original Bill of Rights was a product of eighteenth century philosophy, eighteenth century experiences, and eighteenth century views of the potential and basic nature of man. The draftsmen essentially were motivated by what they feared tyrannical central government could do to them. Today, one lives in a world in which most men and women are more concerned with what the state might do for them. They are concerned with the constitutional recognition of such rights as the rights to employment, to health care, to comprehensive economic security, to a college or post-graduate education.

Yet, the genius of our present system of constitutional rights is that it has successfully met the needs and challenges of each new generation of Americans. Today, its promises seem more vital, more important, than in any past period. Perhaps this is because the components of our society—economics, technology, social structure—have become so complex, so intermingled, that they sometimes seem to threaten to destroy the most important ingredient of a democracy—the individual. No program of government, no service or benefit, can be more important than the preservation of the integrity of human freedom. The private and public sectors are blending into each other at a tremendous pace—privacy is becoming more and more difficult to maintain. The old frontier is gone, so that that plaint "Stop the world, I want to get off!" no longer sounds so facetious.

While all of these factors, and more, conspire to make Americans conform, there was never a greater need than now for differences, for creative people who can furnish the answers that the American society must find if it is to survive.

In the past decade, the work of the Supreme Court in applying and interpreting the basic guarantees of the Bill of Rights and in affirmatively intervening to fill those gaps in the American system which are eroding its foundations has expanded the rights and freedoms of all Americans. In the areas of racial equality, freedom of expression, political effectiveness for all, religious freedom, and the rights of persons charged with crime, the Supreme Court has moved in an ever-broadening circle to protect the rights of ordinary people.

A democracy is the most difficult system of government ever devised. Yet, it is also the most rewarding. It is predicated on the idea that ordinary men and women are capable of governing themselves—of directing their own lives. It compliments its ordinary citizens by assuming that they have the capacities for such responsibility.

Neither the Constitution nor the Supreme Court can insure our civil rights, our basic liberties. The Court uses its best judgment to balance majority rule against minority rights in the difficult cases which it is called upon to decide.

In the last analysis, however, Peter Dunne was not too far from the mark when he wryly observed that the Supreme Court follows the election returns. Certainly, its justices must ultimately find validation for their pronouncements of public policy in the sound opinion of the public—the ultimate authority in a democracy.

For this reason, it is disquieting to learn from published results of public opinion polls that substantial numbers of Americans favor such measures as strict censorship, limitation of free speech, liberal wiretapping, and arbitrary determination of criminal guilt. A study conducted at Purdue University revealed that 83 percent of teen-agers were in favor of wiretapping; 58 percent approved of third-degree methods by the police; 60 percent accepted censorship of books, periodicals, and newspapers; and 25 percent felt it proper for the police to enter a home without a search warrant. There is basis for the belief that adults would be even more emphatic in these views.

In commenting on the role of the Supreme Court in the field of civil rights, Anthony Lewis once observed that the Court has served to "vindicate a demand of national conscience" which "had found no way to express itself, except through the Supreme Court." In the last analysis, only the expressed demand of the community can support the cause of freedom. And, unless the men, women, and children of America believe passionately in the cause of equality and freedom, American democracy cannot survive.

Appendix

THE CONSTITUTION OF THE UNITED STATES

WE THE PEOPLE of the United States, in Order to form a more perfect Union, establish Justice, insure domestic Tranquility, provide for the common defence, promote the general Welfare, and secure the Blessings of Liberty to ourselves and our Posterity, do ordain and establish this Constitution for the United States of America.

ARTICLE I.

SECTION. 1. All legislative Powers herein granted shall be vested in a Congress of the United States, which shall consist of a Senate and House of Representatives.

SECTION. 2. [1] The House of Representatives shall be composed of Members chosen every second Year by the People of the several States, and the Electors in each State shall have the Qualifications requisite for Electors of the most numerous Branch of the State Legislature.

[2] No person shall be a Representative who shall not have attained to the Age of twenty five Years, and been seven Years a Citizen of the United States, and who shall not, when elected, be an Inhabitant of that State in which he shall be chosen.

[3] [Representatives and direct Taxes shall be apportioned among the several States which may be included within this Union, according to their respective Numbers, which shall be determined by adding to the whole Number of free Persons, including those bound to Service for a Term of Years, and excluding Indians not taxed, three fifths of all other Persons.]* The actual Enumeration shall be made within three Years after the first Meeting of the Congress of the United States, and within every subsequent Term of ten Years, in such Manner as they shall by Law direct. The Number of Representatives shall not exceed one for every thirty Thousand, but each State shall have at Least one Representative; and until such enumeration shall be made, the State of New Hampshire shall be entitled to chuse three, Massachusetts eight, Rhode-Island and Providence Plantations one, Connecticut five, New-York six, New Jersey four, Pennsylvania eight, Delaware one, Maryland six, Virginia ten, North Carolina five, South Carolina five, and Georgia three.

[4] When vacancies happen in the Representation from any State, the Executive Authority thereof shall issue Writs of Election to fill such Vacancies.

[5] The House of Representatives shall chuse their Speaker and other Officers; and shall have the sole Power of Impeachment.

NOTE.—This text of the Constitution follows the engrossed copy signed by Gen. Washington and the deputies from 12 States. The superior number preceding the paragraphs designates the number of the clause; it was not in the original.

*The part included in heavy brackets was changed by section 2 of the fourteenth amendment.

SECTION. 3. ¹ The Senate of the United States shall be composed of two Senators from each State, ⟦chosen by the Legislature thereof,⟧* for six Years; and each Senator shall have one Vote.

² Immediately after they shall be assembled in Consequence of the first Election, they shall be divided as equally as may be into three Classes. The Seats of the Senators of the first Class shall be vacated at the Expiration of the second Year, of the second Class at the Expiration of the fourth Year, and of the third Class at the Expiration of the sixth Year, so that one third may be chosen every second Year; ⟦and if Vacancies happen by Resignation, or otherwise, during the Recess of the Legislature of any State, the Executive thereof may make temporary Appointments until the next Meeting of the Legislature, which shall then fill such Vacancies⟧.**

³ No Person shall be a Senator who shall not have attained to the Age of thirty Years, and been nine Years a Citizen of the United States, and who shall not, when elected, be an Inhabitant of that State for which he shall be chosen.

⁴ The Vice President of the United States shall be President of the Senate, but shall have no Vote, unless they be equally divided.

⁵ The Senate shall chuse their other Officers, and also a President pro tempore, in the Absence of the Vice President, or when he shall exercise the Office of President of the United States.

⁶ The Senate shall have the sole Power to try all Impeachments. When sitting for that Purpose, they shall be on Oath or Affirmation. When the President of the United States is tried, the Chief Justice shall preside: And no Person shall be convicted without the Concurrence of two thirds of the Members present.

⁷ Judgment in Cases of Impeachment shall not extend further than to removal from Office, and disqualification to hold and enjoy any Office of honor, Trust or Profit under the United States: but the Party convicted shall nevertheless be liable and subject to Indictment, Trial, Judgment and Punishment, according to Law.

SECTION. 4. ¹ The Times, Places and Manner of holding Elections for Senators and Representatives, shall be prescribed in each State by the Legislature thereof; but the Congress may at any time by Law make or alter such Regulations, except as to the Places of chusing Senators.

² The Congress shall assemble at least once in every Year, and such Meeting shall ⟦be on the first Monday in December,⟧*** unless they shall by Law appoint a different Day.

SECTION. 5. ¹ Each House shall be the Judge of the Elections, Returns and Qualifications of its own Members, and a Majority of each shall constitute a Quorum to do Business; but a smaller Number may adjourn from day to day, and may be authorized to compel the Attendance of absent Members, in such Manner, and under such Penalties as each House may provide.

² Each House may determine the Rules of its Proceedings, punish its Members for disorderly Behaviour, and, with the Concurrence of two thirds, expel a Member.

³ Each House shall keep a Journal of its Proceedings, and from time to time publish the same, excepting such Parts as may in their Judg-

---

*The part included in heavy brackets was changed by section 1 of the seventeenth amendment.
**The part included in heavy brackets was changed by clause 2 of the seventeenth amendment.
***The part included in heavy brackets was changed by section 2 of the twentieth amendment.

ment require Secrecy; and the Yeas and Nays of the Members of either House on any question shall, at the Desire of one fifth of those Present, be entered on the Journal.

⁴ Neither House, during the Session of Congress, shall, without the Consent of the other, adjourn for more than three days, nor to any other Place than that in which the two Houses shall be sitting.

SECTION. 6. ¹ The Senators and Representatives shall receive a Compensation for their Services, to be ascertained by Law, and paid out of the Treasury of the United States. They shall in all Cases, except Treason, Felony and Breach of the Peace, be privileged from Arrest during their Attendance at the Session of their respective Houses, and in going to and returning from the same; and for any Speech or Debate in either House, they shall not be questioned in any other Place.

² No Senator or Representative shall, during the Time for which he was elected, be appointed to any civil Office under the Authority of the United States, which shall have been created, or the Emoluments whereof shall have been encreased during such time; and no Person holding any Office under the United States, shall be a Member of either House during his Continuance in Office.

SECTION. 7. ¹ All Bills for raising Revenue shall originate in the House of Representatives; but the Senate may propose or concur with Amendments as on other Bills.

² Every Bill which shall have passed the House of Representatives and the Senate, shall, before it become a Law, be presented to the President of the United States; If he approve he shall sign it, but if not he shall return it, with his Objections to that House in which it shall have originated, who shall enter the Objections at large on their Journal, and proceed to reconsider it. If after such Reconsideration two thirds of that House shall agree to pass the Bill, it shall be sent, together with the Objections, to the other House, by which it shall likewise be reconsidered, and if approved by two thirds of that House, it shall become a Law. But in all such Cases the Votes of both Houses shall be determined by yeas and Nays, and the Names of the Persons voting for and against the Bill shall be entered on the Journal of each House respectively. If any Bill shall not be returned by the President within ten Days (Sundays excepted) after it shall have been presented to him, the Same shall be a Law, in like Manner as if he had signed it, unless the Congress by their Adjournment prevent its Return, in which Case it shall not be a Law.

³ Every Order, Resolution, or Vote to which the Concurrence of the Senate and House of Representatives may be necessary (except on a question of Adjournment) shall be presented to the President of the United States; and before the Same shall take Effect, shall be approved by him, or being disapproved by him, shall be repassed by two thirds of the Senate and House of Representatives, according to the Rules and Limitations prescribed in the Case of a Bill.

SECTION. 8. ¹ The Congress shall have Power To lay and collect Taxes, Duties, Imposts and Excises, to pay the Debts and provide for the common Defence and general Welfare of the United States; but all Duties, Imposts and Excises shall be uniform throughout the United States;

² To borrow Money on the credit of the United States;

³ To regulate Commerce with foreign Nations, and among the several States, and with the Indian Tribes;

⁴ To establish an uniform Rule of Naturalization, and uniform Laws on the subject of Bankruptcies throughout the United States;

⁵ To coin Money, regulate the Value thereof, and of foreign Coin, and fix the Standard of Weights and Measures;

⁶ To provide for the Punishment of counterfeiting the Securities and current Coin of the United States;

⁷ To establish Post Offices and post Roads;

⁸ To promote the Progress of Science and useful Arts, by securing for limited Times to Authors and Inventors the exclusive Right to their respective Writings and Discoveries;

⁹ To constitute Tribunals inferior to the supreme Court;

¹⁰ To define and punish Piracies and Felonies committed on the high Seas, and Offences against the Law of Nations;

¹¹ To declare War, grant Letters of Marque and Reprisal, and make Rules concerning Captures on Land and Water;

¹² To raise and support Armies, but no Appropriation of Money to that Use shall be for a longer Term than two Years;

¹³ To provide and maintain a Navy;

¹⁴ To make Rules for the Government and Regulation of the land and naval Forces;

¹⁵ To provide for calling forth the Militia to execute the Laws of the Union, suppress Insurrections and repel Invasions;

¹⁶ To provide for organizing, arming, and disciplining, the Militia, and for governing such Part of them as may be employed in the Service of the United States, reserving to the States respectively, the Appointment of the Officers, and the Authority of training the Militia according to the discipline prescribed by Congress;

¹⁷ To exercise exclusive Legislation in all Cases whatsoever, over such District (not exceeding ten Miles square) as may, by Cession of particular States, and the Acceptance of Congress, become the Seat of the Government of the United States, and to exercise like Authority over all Places purchased by the Consent of the Legislature of the State in which the Same shall be, for the Erection of Forts, Magazines, Arsenals, dock-Yards, and other needful Buildings;—And

¹⁸ To make all Laws which shall be necessary and proper for carrying into Execution the foregoing Powers, and all other Powers vested by this Constitution in the Government of the United States, or in any Department or Officer thereof.

SECTION. 9. ¹ The Migration or Importation of such Persons as any of the States now existing shall think proper to admit, shall not be prohibited by the Congress prior to the Year one thousand eight hundred and eight, but a Tax or duty may be imposed on such Importation, not exceeding ten dollars for each Person.

² The Privilege of the Writ of Habeas Corpus shall not be suspended, unless when in Cases of Rebellion or Invasion the public Safety may require it.

³ No Bill of Attainder or ex post facto Law shall be passed.

*⁴ No Capitation, or other direct, Tax shall be laid, unless in Proportion to the Census or Enumeration herein before directed to be taken.

⁵ No Tax or Duty shall be laid on Articles exported from any State.

*See also the sixteenth amendment.

⁶ No Preference shall be given by any Regulation of Commerce or Revenue to the Ports of one State over those of another: nor shall Vessels bound to, or from, one State, be obliged to enter, clear, or pay Duties in another.

⁷ No Money shall be drawn from the Treasury, but in Consequence of Appropriations made by Law; and a regular Statement and Account of the Receipts and Expenditures of all public Money shall be published from time to time.

⁸ No Title of Nobility shall be granted by the United States: And no Person holding any Office of Profit or Trust under them, shall, without the Consent of the Congress, accept of any present, Emolument, Office, or Title, of any kind whatever, from any King, Prince, or foreign State.

SECTION. 10. ¹ No State shall enter into any Treaty, Alliance, or Confederation; grant Letters of Marque and Reprisal; coin Money; emit Bills of Credit; make any Thing but gold and silver Coin a Tender in Payment of Debts; pass any Bill of Attainder, ex post facto Law, or Law impairing the Obligation of Contracts, or grant any Title of Nobility.

² No State shall, without the Consent of the Congress, lay any Imposts or Duties on Imports or Exports, except what may be absolutely necessary for executing it's inspection Laws: and the net Produce of all Duties and Imposts, laid by any State on Imports or Exports, shall be for the Use of the Treasury of the United States; and all such Laws shall be subject to the Revision and Controul of the Congress.

³ No State shall, without the Consent of Congress, lay any Duty of Tonnage, keep Troops, or Ships of War in time of Peace, enter into any Agreement or Compact with another State, or with a foreign Power, or engage in War, unless actually invaded, or in such imminent Danger as will not admit of delay.

ARTICLE II.

SECTION. 1. ¹ The executive Power shall be vested in a President of the United States of America. He shall hold his Office during the Term of four Years, and, together with the Vice President, chosen for the same Term, be elected, as follows

² Each State shall appoint, in such Manner as the Legislature thereof may direct, a Number of Electors, equal to the whole Number of Senators and Representatives to which the State may be entitled in the Congress: but no Senator or Representative, or Person holding an Office of Trust or Profit under the United States, shall be appointed an Elector.

⟦The Electors shall meet in their respective States, and vote by Ballot for two Persons, of whom one at least shall not be an Inhabitant of the same State with themselves. And they shall make a List of all the Persons voted for, and of the Number of Votes for each; which List they shall sign and certify, and transmit sealed to the Seat of the Government of the United States, directed to the President of the Senate. The President of the Senate shall, in the Presence of the Senate and House of Representatives, open all the Certificates, and the Votes shall then be counted. The Person having the greatest

Number of Votes shall be the President, if such Number be a Majority of the whole Number of Electors appointed; and if there be more than one who have such Majority, and have an equal Number of Votes, then the House of Representatives shall immediately chuse by Ballot one of them for President; and if no Person have a Majority, then from the five highest on the List the said House shall in like Manner chuse the President. But in chusing the President, the Votes shall be taken by States, the Representation from each State having one Vote; A quorum for this Purpose shall consist of a Member or Members from two thirds of the States, and a Majority of all the States shall be necessary to a Choice. In every Case, after the Choice of the President, the Person having the greatest Number of Votes of the Electors shall be the Vice President. But if there should remain two or more who have equal Votes, the Senate shall chuse from them by Ballot the Vice President.]*

[3] The Congress may determine the Time of chusing the Electors, and the Day on which they shall give their Votes; which Day shall be the same throughout the United States.

[4] No Person except a natural born Citizen, or a Citizen of the United States, at the time of the Adoption of this Constitution, shall be eligible to the Office of President; neither shall any Person be eligible to that Office who shall not have attained to the Age of thirty five Years, and been fourteen Years a Resident within the United States.

[5] In Case of the Removal of the President from Office, or of his Death, Resignation, or Inability to discharge the Powers and Duties of the said Office,† the Same shall devolve on the Vice President, and the Congress may by Law provide for the Case of Removal, Death, Resignation or Inability, both of the President and Vice President, declaring what Officer shall then act as President, and such Officer shall act accordingly, until the Disability be removed, or a President shall be elected.

[6] The President shall, at stated Times, receive for his Services, a Compensation, which shall neither be encreased nor diminished during the Period for which he shall have been elected, and he shall not receive within that Period any other Emolument from the United States, or any of them.

[7] Before he enter on the Execution of his Office, he shall take the following Oath or Affirmation:—"I do solemnly swear (or affirm) that I will faithfully execute the Office of President of the United States, and will to the best of my Ability, preserve, protect and defend the Constitution of the United States."

SECTION. 2. [1] The President shall be Commander in Chief of the Army and Navy of the United States, and of the Militia of the several States, when called into the actual Service of the United States; he may require the Opinion, in writing, of the principal Officer in each of the executive Departments, upon any Subject relating to the Duties of their respective Offices, and he shall have Power to grant Reprieves and Pardons for Offences against the United States, except in Cases of Impeachment.

[2] He shall have Power, by and with the Advice and Consent of the Senate, to make Treaties, provided two thirds of the Senators present concur; and he shall nominate, and by and with the Advice and Con-

---

*This paragraph has been superseded by the twelfth amendment.
†This provision has been affected by the twenty-fifth amendment.

sent of the Senate, shall appoint Ambassadors, other public Ministers and Consuls, Judges of the supreme Court, and all other Officers of the United States, whose Appointments are not herein otherwise provided for, and which shall be established by Law: but the Congress may by Law vest the Appointment of such inferior Officers, as they think proper, in the President alone, in the Courts of Law, or in the Heads of Departments.

³ The President shall have Power to fill up all Vacancies that may happen during the Recess of the Senate, by granting Commissions which shall expire at the End of their next Session.

SECTION. 3. He shall from time to time give to the Congress Information of the State of the Union, and recommend to their Consideration such Measures as he shall judge necessary and expedient; he may, on extraordinary Occasions, convene both Houses, or either of them, and in Case of Disagreement between them, with Respect to the Time of Adjournment, he may adjourn them to such Time as he shall think proper; he shall receive Ambassadors and other public Ministers; he shall take Care that the Laws be faithfully executed, and shall Commission all the Officers of the United States.

SECTION. 4. The President, Vice President and all civil Officers of the United States, shall be removed from Office on Impeachment for, and Conviction of, Treason, Bribery, or other high Crimes and Misdemeanors.

ARTICLE III.

SECTION. 1. The judicial Power of the United States, shall be vested in one supreme Court, and in such inferior Courts as the Congress may from time to time ordain and establish. The Judges, both of the supreme and inferior Courts, shall hold their Offices during good Behaviour, and shall, at stated Times, receive for their Services, a Compensation, which shall not be diminished during their Continuance in Office.

SECTION. 2. ¹ The judicial Power shall extend to all Cases, in Law and Equity, arising under this Constitution, the Laws of the United States, and Treaties made, or which shall be made, under their Authority;—to all Cases affecting Ambassadors, other public Ministers and Consuls;—to all Cases of admiralty and maritime Jurisdiction;—to Controversies to which the United States shall be a Party;—to Controversies between two or more States;—between a State and Citizens of another State;*—between Citizens of different States,—between Citizens of the same State claiming Lands under Grants of different States, and between a State, or the Citizens thereof, and foreign States, Citizens or Subjects.

² In all Cases affecting Ambassadors, other public Ministers and Consuls, and those in which a State shall be Party, the supreme Court shall have original Jurisdiction. In all the other Cases before mentioned, the supreme Court shall have appellate Jurisdiction, both as to Law and Fact, with such Exceptions, and under such Regulations as the Congress shall make.

³ The Trial of all Crimes, except in Cases of Impeachment, shall be by Jury; and such Trial shall be held in the State where the said Crimes shall have been committed; but when not committed within any State,

---

*This clause has been affected by the eleventh amendment.

the Trial shall be at such Place or Places as the Congress may by Law have directed.

SECTION. 3. [1] Treason against the United States, shall consist only in levying War against them, or in adhering to their Enemies, giving them Aid and Comfort. No Person shall be convicted of Treason unless on the Testimony of two Witnesses to the same overt Act, or on Confession in open Court.

[2] The Congress shall have Power to declare the Punishment of Treason, but no Attainder of Treason shall work Corruption of Blood, or Forfeiture except during the Life of the Person attainted.

ARTICLE IV.

SECTION. 1. Full Faith and Credit shall be given in each State to the public Acts, Records, and judicial Proceedings of every other State. And the Congress may by general Laws prescribe the Manner in which such Acts, Records and Proceedings shall be proved, and the Effect thereof.

SECTION. 2. [1] The Citizens of each State shall be entitled to all Privileges and Immunities of Citizens in the several States.

[2] A Person charged in any State with Treason, Felony, or other Crime, who shall flee from Justice, and be found in another State, shall on Demand of the executive Authority of the State from which he fled, be delivered up, to be removed to the State having Jurisdiction of the Crime.

[3] [No Person held to Service or Labour in one State, under the Laws thereof, escaping into another, shall, in Consequence of any Law or Regulation therein, be discharged from such Service or Labour, but shall be delivered up on Claim of the Party to whom such Service or Labour may be due.]*

SECTION. 3. [1] New States may be admitted by the Congress into this Union; but no new State shall be formed or erected within the Jurisdiction of any other State; nor any State be formed by the Junction of two or more States, or Parts of States, without the Consent of the Legislatures of the States concerned as well as of the Congress.

[2] The Congress shall have Power to dispose of and make all needful Rules and Regulations respecting the Territory or other Property belonging to the United States; and nothing in this Constitution shall be so construed as to Prejudice any Claims of the United States, or of any particular State.

SECTION. 4. The United States shall guarantee to every State in this Union a Republican Form of Government, and shall protect each of them against Invasion; and on Application of the Legislature, or of the Executive (when the Legislature cannot be convened) against domestic Violence.

ARTICLE V.

The Congress, whenever two thirds of both Houses shall deem it necessary, shall propose Amendments to this Constitution, or, on the Application of the Legislatures of two thirds of the several States, shall call a Convention for proposing Amendments, which, in either Case, shall be valid to all Intents and Purposes, as Part of this Constitution, when ratified by the Legislatures of three fourths of the

---

*This paragraph has been superseded by the thirteenth amendment.

several States, or by Conventions in three fourths thereof, as the one or the other Mode of Ratification may be proposed by the Congress; Provided [that no Amendment which may be made prior to the Year One thousand eight hundred and eight shall in any Manner affect the first and fourth Clauses in the Ninth Section of the first Article; and]* that no State, without its Consent, shall be deprived of its equal Suffrage in the Senate.

ARTICLE VI.

[1] All Debts contracted and Engagements entered into, before the Adoption of this Constitution, shall be as valid against the United States under this Constitution, as under the Confederation.

[2] This Constitution, and the Laws of the United States which shall be made in Pursuance thereof; and all Treaties made, or which shall be made, under the Authority of the United States, shall be the supreme Law of the Land; and the Judges in every State shall be bound thereby, any Thing in the Constitution or Laws of any State to the Contrary notwithstanding.

[3] The Senators and Representatives before mentioned, and the Members of the several State Legislatures, and all executive and judicial Officers, both of the United States and of the several States, shall be bound by Oath or Affirmation, to support this Constitution; but no religious Test shall ever be required as a Qualification to any Office or public Trust under the United States.

ARTICLE VII.

The Ratification of the Conventions of nine States, shall be sufficient for the Establishment of this Constitution between the States so ratifying the Same.

DONE in Convention by the Unanimous Consent of the States present the Seventeenth Day of September in the Year of our Lord one thousand seven hundred and Eighty seven and of the Independence of the United States of America the Twelfth   IN WITNESS whereof We have hereunto subscribed our Names,

AMENDMENTS TO THE CONSTITUTION

ARTICLE I. *

Congress shall make no law respecting an establishment of religion, or prohibiting the free exercise thereof; or abridging the freedom of speech, or of the press; or the right of the people peaceably to assemble, and to petition the Government for a redress of grievances.

ARTICLE II.

A well regulated Militia, being necessary to the security of a free State, the right of the people to keep and bear Arms, shall not be infringed.

ARTICLE III.

No Soldier shall, in time of peace be quartered in any house, without the consent of the Owner, nor in time of war, but in a manner to be prescribed by law.

ARTICLE IV.

The right of the people to be secure in their persons, houses, papers, and effects, against unreasonable searches and seizures, shall not be violated, and no Warrants shall issue, but upon probable cause, supported by Oath or affirmation, and particularly describing the place to be searched, and the persons or things to be seized.

ARTICLE V.

No person shall be held to answer for a capital, or otherwise infamous crime, unless on a presentment or indictment of a Grand Jury, except in cases arising in the land or naval forces, or in the Militia, when in actual service in time of War or public danger; nor shall any person be subject for the same offence to be twice put in jeopardy of life or limb; nor shall be compelled in any criminal case to be a witness against himself, nor be deprived of life, liberty, or property, without due process of law; nor shall private property be taken for public use without just compensation.

ARTICLE VI.

In all criminal prosecutions, the accused shall enjoy the right to a speedy and public trial, by an impartial jury of the State and district wherein the crime shall have been committed, which district shall

---

*Only the 13th, 14th, 15th, and 16th articles of amendment had numbers assigned to them at the time of ratification.

have been previously ascertained by law, and to be informed of the nature and cause of the accusation; to be confronted with the witnesses against him; to have compulsory process for obtaining Witnesses in his favor, and to have the assistance of counsel for his defence.

ARTICLE VII.

In Suits at common law, where the value in controversy shall exceed twenty dollars, the right of trial by jury shall be preserved, and no fact tried by a jury, shall be otherwise reexamined in any Court of the United States, than according to the rules of the common law.

ARTICLE VIII.

Excessive bail shall not be required, nor excessive fines imposed, nor cruel and unusual punishments inflicted.

ARTICLE IX.

The enumeration in the Constitution, of certain rights, shall not be construed to deny or disparage others retained by the people.

ARTICLE X.

The powers not delegated to the United States by the Constitution, nor prohibited by it to the States, are reserved to the States respectively, or to the people.

The first 10 amendments to the Constitution, and 2 others that failed of ratification, were proposed by the Congress on September 25, 1789. They were ratified by the following States, and the notifications of the ratification by the Governors thereof were successively communicated by the President to the Congress: New Jersey, November 20, 1789; Maryland, December 19, 1789; North Carolina, December 22, 1789; South Carolina, January 19, 1790; New Hampshire, January 25, 1790; Delaware, January 28, 1790; New York, February 24, 1790; Pennsylvania, March 10, 1790; Rhode Island, June 7, 1790; Vermont, November 3, 1791; and Virginia, December 15, 1791.

Ratification was completed on December 15, 1791.

The amendments were subsequently ratified by Massachusetts, March 2, 1939; Connecticut, April 19, 1939; and Georgia, March 18, 1939.

ARTICLE XI.

The Judicial power of the United States shall not be construed to extend to any suit in law or equity, commenced or prosecuted against one of the United States by Citizens of another State, or by Citizens or Subjects of any Foreign State.

The 11th amendment to the Constitution was proposed by the Congress on March 4, 1794. It was declared, in a message from the President to Congress, dated January 8, 1798 to have been ratified by the legislatures of 12 of the 15 States. The dates of ratification were: New York, March 27, 1794; Rhode Island, March 31, 1794; Connecticut, May 8, 1794; New Hampshire, June 16, 1794; Massachusetts, June 26, 1794; Vermont, between October 9, 1794 and November 9, 1794; Virginia, November 18, 1794; Georgia, November 29, 1794; Kentucky, December 7, 1794; Maryland, December 26, 1794; Delaware, January 23, 1795; North Carolina, February 7, 1795.

Ratification was completed on February 7, 1795.

The amendment was subsequently ratified by South Carolina on December 4, 1797. New Jersey and Pennsylvania did not take action on the amendment.

ARTICLE XII.

The electors shall meet in their respective states and vote by ballot for President and Vice-President, one of whom, at least, shall not be an inhabitant of the same state with themselves; they shall name in their ballots the person voted for as President, and in distinct ballots the person voted for as Vice-President, and they shall make distinct lists of all persons voted for as President, and of all persons voted for as Vice-President, and of the number of votes for each, which lists they shall sign and certify, and transmit sealed to the seat of the government of the United States, directed to the President of the Senate;— The President of the Senate shall, in the presence of the Senate and House of Representatives, open all the certificates and the votes shall then be counted;—The person having the greatest number of votes for President, shall be the President, if such number be a majority of the whole number of Electors appointed; and if no person have such majority, then from the persons having the highest numbers not exceeding three on the list of those voted for as President, the House of Representatives shall choose immediately, by ballot, the President. But in choosing the President, the votes shall be taken by states, the representation from each state having one vote; a quorum for this purpose shall consist of a member or members from two-thirds of the states, and a majority of all the states shall be necessary to a choice. [And if the House of Representatives shall not choose a President whenever the right of choice shall devolve upon them, before the fourth day of March next following, then the Vice-President shall act as President, as in the case of the death or other constitutional disability of the President.]* The person having the greatest number of votes as Vice-President, shall be the Vice-President, if such number be a majority of the whole number of Electors appointed, and if no person have a majority, then from the two highest numbers on the list, the Senate shall choose the Vice-President; a quorum for the purpose shall consist of two-thirds of the whole number of Senators, and a majority of the whole number shall be necessary to a choice. But no person constitutionally ineligible to the office of President shall be eligible to that of Vice-President of the United States.

The 12th amendment to the Constitution was proposed by the Congress on December 9, 1803. It was declared, in a proclamation of the Secretary of State, dated September 25, 1804, to have been ratified by the legislatures of 13 of the 17 States. The dates of ratification were: Vermont, October 28, 1803; North Carolina, December 21, 1803; Maryland, December 24, 1803; Kentucky, December 27, 1803; Ohio, December 30, 1803; Pennsylvania, January 5, 1804; Virginia, February 3, 1804; New York, February 10, 1804; New Jersey, February 22, 1804; Rhode Island, March 12, 1804; South Carolina, May 15, 1804; Georgia, May 19, 1804; New Hampshire, June 15, 1804.
Ratification was completed on June 15, 1804.
The amendment was subsequently ratified by Tennessee, July 27, 1804.
The amendment was rejected by Delaware, January 18, 1804; Massachusetts, February 2 or 3, 1804; Connecticut, at its session begun May 10, 1804.

ARTICLE XIII.

Section 1. Neither slavery nor involuntary servitude, except as a punishment for crime whereof the party shall have been duly con-

*The part included in heavy brackets has been superseded by section 3 of the twentieth amendment.

victed, shall exist within the United States, or any place subject to their jurisdiction.

SECTION 2. Congress shall have power to enforce this article by appropriate legislation.

The 13th amendment to the Constitution was proposed by the Congress on January 31, 1865. It was declared, in a proclamation of the Secretary of State, dated December 18, 1865, to have been ratified by the legislatures of 27 of the 36 States. The dates of ratification were: Illinois, February 1, 1865; Rhode Island, February 2, 1865; Michigan, February 2, 1865; Maryland, February 3, 1865; New York, February 3, 1865; Pennsylvania, February 3, 1865: West Virginia, February 3, 1865; Missouri, February 6, 1865; Maine, February 7, 1865; Kansas, February 7, 1865; Massachusetts, February 7, 1865; Virginia, February 9, 1865; Ohio, February 10, 1865; Indiana, February 13, 1865; Nevada, February 16, 1865; Louisiana, February 17, 1865; Minnesota, February 23, 1865; Wisconsin, February 24, 1865; Vermont, March 9, 1865; Tennessee, April 7, 1865; Arkansas, April 14, 1865; Connecticut, May 4, 1865; New Hampshire, July 1, 1865; South Carolina, November 13, 1865; Alabama, December 2, 1865; North Carolina, December 4, 1865; Georgia, December 6, 1865.

Ratification was completed on December 6, 1865.

The amendment was subsequently ratified by Oregon, December 8, 1865; California, December 19, 1865; Florida, December 28, 1865 (Florida again ratified on June 9, 1868, upon its adoption of a new constitution); Iowa, January 15, 1866; New Jersey, January 23, 1866 (after having rejected the amendment on March 16, 1865); Texas, February 18, 1870; Delaware, February 12, 1901 (after having rejected the amendment on February 8, 1865).

The amendment was rejected by Kentucky, February 24, 1865, and by Mississippi, December 4, 1865.

ARTICLE XIV.

SECTION 1. All persons born or naturalized in the United States, and subject to the jurisdiction thereof, are citizens of the United States and of the State wherein they reside. No State shall make or enforce any law which shall abridge the privileges or immunities of citizens of the United States; nor shall any State deprive any person of life, liberty, or property, without due process of law; nor deny to any person within its jurisdiction the equal protection of the laws.

SECTION 2. Representatives shall be apportioned among the several States according to their respective numbers, counting the whole number of persons in each State, excluding Indians not taxed. But when the right to vote at any election for the choice of electors for President and Vice President of the United States, Representatives in Congress, the Executive and Judicial officers of a State, or the members of the Legislature thereof, is denied to any of the male inhabitants of such State, being twenty-one years of age, and citizens of the United States, or in any way abridged, except for participation in rebellion, or other crime, the basis of representation therein shall be reduced in the proportion which the number of such male citizens shall bear to the whole number of male citizens twenty-one years of age in such State.

SECTION 3. No person shall be a Senator or Representative in Congress, or elector of President and Vice President, or hold any office, civil or military, under the United States, or under any State, who, having previously taken an oath, as a member of Congress, or as an officer of the United States, or as a member of any State legislature, or as an executive or judicial officer of any State, to support the Constitution of the United States, shall have engaged in insurrection or rebellion against the same, or given aid or comfort to the enemies thereof. But Congress may by a vote of two-thirds of each House, remove such disability.

SECTION 4. The validity of the public debt of the United States, authorized by law, including debts incurred for payment of pensions and bounties for services in suppressing insurrection or rebellion, shall not be questioned. But neither the United States nor any State shall assume or pay any debt or obligation incurred in aid of insurrection or rebellion against the United States, or any claim for the loss or emancipation of any slave; but all such debts, obligations and claims shall be held illegal and void.

SECTION 5. The Congress shall have power to enforce, by appropriate legislation, the provisions of this article.

The 14th amendment to the Constitution was proposed by the Congress on June 13, 1866. It was declared, in a certificate by the Secretary of State dated July 28, 1868, to have been ratified by the legislatures of 28 of the 37 States. The dates of ratification were: Connecticut, June 25, 1866;. New Hampshire, July 6, 1866; Tennessee, July 19, 1866; New Jersey, September 11, 1866 (subsequently the legislature rescinded its ratification, and on March 5, 1868, re-adopted its resolution of rescission over the Governor's veto); Oregon, September 19, 1866 (and rescinded its ratification on October 15, 1868); Vermont, October 30, 1866; Ohio, January 4, 1867 (and rescinded its ratification on January 15, 1868); New York, January 10, 1867; Kansas, January 11, 1867; Illinois, January 15, 1867; West Virginia, January 16, 1867; Michigan, January 16, 1867; Minnesota, January 16, 1867; Maine, January 19, 1867; Nevada, January 22, 1867; Indiana, January 23, 1867; Missouri, January 25, 1867; Rhode Island, February 7, 1867; Wisconsin, February 7, 1867; Pennsylvania, February 12, 1867; Massachusetts, March 20, 1867; Nebraska, June 15, 1867; Iowa, March 16, 1868; Arkansas, April 6, 1868; Florida, June 9, 1868; North Carolina, July 4, 1868 (after having rejected it on December 14, 1866); Louisiana, July 9, 1868 (after having rejected it on February 6, 1867); South Carolina, July 9, 1868 (after having rejected it on December 20, 1866).

Ratification was completed on July 9, 1868.[1]

The amendment was subsequently ratified by Alabama, July 13 ,1868; Georgia, July 21, 1868 (after having rejected it on November 9, 1866); Virginia, October 8, 1869 (after having rejected it on January 9, 1867); Mississippi, January 17, 1870; Texas, February 18, 1870 (after having rejected it on October 27, 1866); Delaware, February 12, 1901 (after having rejected it on February 8, 1867); Maryland, April 4, 1959 (after having rejected it on March 23, 1867); California, May 6, 1959.

ARTICLE XV.

SECTION 1. The right of citizens of the United States to vote shall not be denied or abridged by the United States or by any State on account of race, color, or previous condition of servitude.

SECTION 2. The Congress shall have power to enforce this article by appropriate legislation.

The 15th amendment to the Constitution was proposed by the Congress on February 26, 1869. It was declared, in a proclamation of the Secretary of State, dated March 30, 1870, to have been ratified by the legislatures of 29 of the 37 States. The dates of ratification were: Nevada, March 1, 1869; West Virginia, March 3, 1869; Illinois, March 5, 1869; Louisiana, March 5, 1869; North Carolina, March 5, 1869; Michigan, March 8, 1869; Wisconsin, March 9, 1869; Maine, March 11, 1869; Massachusetts, March 12, 1869; Arkansas, March 15, 1869; South Carolina, March 15, 1869; Pennsylvania, March 25, 1869; New York, April 14, 1869 (and the legislature of the same State passed a resolution January 5, 1870, to withdraw its consent to it); Indiana, May 14, 1869; Connecticut, May 19, 1869; Florida, June 14, 1869; New Hampshire, July 1, 1869; Virginia, October 8, 1869; Vermont, October 20, 1869; Missouri, January 7, 1870; Minnesota, January 13, 1870; Mississippi, January 17, 1870; Rhode Island, January

---

[1] The certificate of the Secretary of State, dated July 20, 1868, was based upon the assumption of invalidity of the rescission of ratification by Ohio and New Jersey. The following day, the Congress adopted a joint resolution declaring the amendment a part of the Constitution. The Secretary of State issued a proclamation of ratification without reservation.

18, 1870; Kansas, January 19, 1870; Ohio, January 27, 1870 (after having rejected it on April 30, 1869); Georgia, February 2, 1870; Iowa, February 3, 1870.

Ratification was completed on February 3, 1870, unless the withdrawal of ratification by New York was effective; in which event ratification was completed on February 17, 1870, when Nebraska ratified.

The amendment was subsequently ratified by Texas, February 18, 1870; New Jersey, February 15, 1871 (after having rejected it on February 7, 1870); Delaware, February 12, 1901 (after having rejected it on March 18, 1869); Oregon, February 24, 1959; California, April 3, 1962 (after having rejected it on January 28, 1870).

ARTICLE XVI.

The Congress shall have power to lay and collect taxes on incomes, from whatever source derived, without apportionment among the several States, and without regard to any census or enumeration.

The 16th amendment to the Constitution was proposed by the Congress on July 12, 1909. It was declared, in a proclamation of the Secretary of State, dated February 25, 1913, to have been ratified by 36 of the 48 States. The dates of ratification were: Alabama, August 10, 1909; Kentucky, February 8, 1910; South Carolina, February 19, 1910; Illinois, March 1, 1910; Mississippi, March 7, 1910; Oklahoma, March 10, 1910; Maryland, April 8, 1910; Georgia, August 3, 1910; Texas, August 16, 1910; Ohio, January 19, 1911; Idaho, January 20, 1911; Oregon, January 23, 1911; Washington, January 26, 1911; Montana, January 30, 1911; Indiana, January 30, 1911; California, January 31, 1911; Nevada, January 31, 1911; South Dakota, February 3, 1911; Nebraska, February 9, 1911; North Carolina, February 11, 1911; Colorado, February 15, 1911; North Dakota, February 17, 1911; Kansas, February 18, 1911; Michigan, February 23, 1911; Iowa, February 24, 1911; Missouri, March 16, 1911; Maine, March 31, 1911; Tennessee, April 7, 1911; Arkansas, April 22, 1911 (after having rejected it earlier); Wisconsin, May 26, 1911; New York, July 12, 1911; Arizona, April 6, 1912; Louisiana, June 28, 1912; Minnesota, July 11, 1912; West Virginia, January 31, 1913; New Mexico, February 3, 1913.

Ratification was completed on February 3, 1913.

The amendment was subsequently ratified by Massachusetts, March 4, 1913; New Hampshire, March 7, 1913 (after having rejected it on March 2, 1911).

The amendment was rejected by Connecticut, Rhode Island, and Utah.

ARTICLE XVII.

The Senate of the United States shall be composed of two Senators from each State, elected by the people thereof, for six years; and each Senator shall have one vote. The electors in each State shall have the qualifications requisite for electors of the most numerous branch of the State legislatures.

When vacancies happen in the representation of any State in the Senate, the executive authority of such State shall issue writs of election to fill such vacancies: *Provided,* That the legislature of any State may empower the executive thereof to make temporary appointments until the people fill the vacancies by election as the legislature may direct.

This amendment shall not be so construed as to affect the election or term of any Senator chosen before it becomes valid as part of the Constitution.

The 17th amendment to the Constitution was proposed by the Congress on May 13, 1912. It was declared, in a proclamation by the Secretary of State, dated May 31, 1913, to have been ratified by the legislatures of 36 of the 48 States. The dates of ratification were: Massachusetts, May 22, 1912; Arizona, June 3, 1912; Minnesota, June 10, 1912; New York, January 15, 1913; Kansas, January 17, 1913; Oregon, January 23, 1913; North Carolina, January 25, 1913; California, January 28, 1913; Michigan, January 28, 1913; Iowa, January 30, 1913; Montana, January 30, 1913; Idaho, January 31, 1913; West Virginia, February 4, 1913; Colorado, February 5, 1913; Nevada, February 6, 1913; Texas,

February 7, 1913; Washington, February 7, 1913; Wyoming, February 8, 1913; Arkansas, February 11, 1913; Maine, February 11, 1913; Illinois, February 13, 1913; North Dakota, February 14, 1913; Wisconsin, February 18, 1913; Indiana, February 19, 1913; New Hampshire, February 19, 1913; Vermont, February 19, 1913; South Dakota, February 19, 1913; Oklahoma, February 24, 1913; Ohio, February 25, 1913; Missouri, March 7, 1913; New Mexico, March 13, 1913; Nebraska, March 14, 1913; New Jersey, March 17, 1913; Tennessee, April 1, 1913; Pennsylvania, April 2, 1913; Connecticut, April 8, 1913.
Ratification was completed on April 8, 1913.
The amendment was subsequently ratified by Louisiana, June 11, 1914.
The amendment was rejected by Utah on February 26, 1913, and by Delaware on March 18, 1913.

ARTICLE XVIII.

[SECTION 1. After one year from the ratification of this article the manufacture, sale, or transportation of intoxicating liquors within, the importation thereof into, or the exportation thereof from the United States and all territory subject to the jurisdiction thereof for beverage purposes is hereby prohibited.
[SECTION 2. The Congress and the several States shall have concurrent power to enforce this article by approriate legislation.
[SECTION 3. This article shall be inoperative unless it shall have been ratified as an amendment to the Constitution by the legislatures of the several States, as provided in the Constitution, within seven years from the date of the submission hereof to the States by the Congress.]*

The 18th amendment to the Constitution was proposed by the Congress on December 18, 1917. It was declared, in a proclamation by the Acting Secretary of State, dated January 29, 1919, to have been ratified by the legislatures of 36 of the 48 States. The dates of ratification were: Mississippi, January 8, 1918; Virginia, January 11, 1918; Kentucky, January 14, 1918; North Dakota, January 25, 1918; South Carolina, January 29, 1918; Maryland, February 13, 1918; Montana, February 19, 1918; Texas, March 4, 1918; Delaware, March 18, 1918; South Dakota, March 20, 1918; Massachusetts, April 2, 1918; Arizona, May 24, 1918; Georgia, June 26, 1918; Louisiana, August 3, 1918; Florida, December 3, 1918; Michigan, January 2, 1919; Ohio, January 7, 1919; Oklahoma, January 7, 1919; Idaho, January 8, 1919; Maine, January 8, 1919; West Virginia, January 9, 1919; California, January 13, 1919; Tennessee, January 13, 1919; Washington, January 13, 1919; Arkansas, January 14, 1919; Kansas, January 14, 1919; Alabama, January 15, 1919; Colorado, January 15, 1919; Iowa, January 15, 1919; New Hampshire, January 15, 1919; Oregon, January 15, 1919; Nebraska, January 16, 1919; North Carolina, January 16, 1919; Utah, January 16, 1919; Missouri, January 16, 1919; Wyoming, January 16, 1919.
Ratification was completed on January 16, 1919.
The amendment was subsequently ratified by Minnesota on January 17, 1917; New Mexico, January 20, 1919; Nevada, January 21, 1919; New York, January 29, 1919; Vermont, January 29, 1919; Pennsylvania, February 25, 1919; Connecticut, May 6, 1919; and New Jersey, March 9, 1922.
The amendment was rejected by Rhode Island.

ARTICLE XIX.

The right of citizens of the United States to vote shall not be denied or abridged by the United States or by any State on account of sex.
Congress shall have power to enforce this article by appropriate legislation.

The 19th amendment to the Constitution was proposed by the Congress on June 4, 1919. It was declared, in a certificate by the Secretary of State, dated

*Repealed by section 1 of the twenty-first amendment.

August 26, 1920, to have been ratified by the legislatures of 36 of the 48 States. The dates of ratification were: Illinois, June 10, 1919 (and that State readopted its resolution of ratification June 17, 1919); Michigan, June 10, 1919; Wisconsin, June 10, 1919; Kansas, June 16, 1919; New York, June 16, 1919; Ohio, June 16, 1919; Pennsylvania, June 24, 1919; Massachusetts, June 25, 1919; Texas, June 28, 1919; Iowa, July 2, 1919; Missouri, July 3, 1919; Arkansas, July 28, 1919; Montana, August 2, 1919; Nebraska, August 2, 1919; Minnesota, September 8, 1919; New Hampshire, September 10, 1919; Utah, October 2, 1919; California, November 1, 1919; Maine, November 5, 1919; North Dakota, December 1, 1919; South Dakota, December 4, 1919; Colorado, December 15, 1919; Kentucky, January 6, 1920; Rhode Island, January 6, 1920; Oregon, January 13, 1920; Indiana, January 16, 1920; Wyoming, January 27, 1920; Nevada, February 7, 1920; New Jersey, February 9, 1920; Idaho, February 11, 1920; Arizona, February 12, 1920; New Mexico, February 21, 1920; Oklahoma, February 28, 1920; West Virginia, March 10, 1920; Washington, March 22, 1920; Tennessee, August 28, 1920.

Ratification was completed on August 20, 1920.

The amendment was subsequently ratified by Connecticut on September 14, 1920 (and that State reaffirmed on September 21, 1920); Vermont, February 8, 1921; Maryland, March 29, 1941 (after having rejected it on February 24, 1920; ratification certified on February 25, 1958); Alabama, September 8, 1953 (after that State had rejected it on September 22, 1919).

The amendment was rejected by Georgia on July 25, 1919; South Carolina, January 28, 1920; Virginia, February 12, 1920; Mississippi, March 29, 1920; Delaware, June 2, 1920; Louisiana, July 1, 1920.

ARTICLE XX.

SECTION 1. The terms of the President and Vice President shall end at noon on the 20th day of January, and the terms of Senators and Representatives at noon on the 3d day of January, of the years in which such terms would have ended if this article had not been ratified; and the terms of their successors shall then begin.

SECTION 2. The Congress shall assemble at least once in every year, and such meeting shall begin at noon on the 3d day of January, unless they shall by law appoint a different day.

SECTION 3. If, at the time fixed for the beginning of the term of the President, the President elect shall have died, the Vice President elect shall become President. If a President shall not have been chosen before the time fixed for the beginning of his term, or if the President elect shall have failed to qualify, then the Vice President elect shall act as President until a President shall have qualified; and the Congress may by law provide for the case wherein neither a President elect nor a Vice President elect shall have qualified, declaring who shall then act as President, or the manner in which one who is to act shall be selected, and such person shall act accordingly until a President or Vice President shall have qualified.

SECTION 4. The Congress may by law provide for the case of the death of any of the persons from whom the House of Representatives may choose a President whenever the right of choice shall have devolved upon them, and for the case of the death of any of the persons from whom the Senate may choose a Vice President whenever the right of choice shall have devolved upon them.

SECTION 5. Sections 1 and 2 shall take effect on the 15th day of October following the ratification of this article.

SECTION 6. This article shall be inoperative unless it shall have been ratified as an amendment to the Constitution by the legislatures of three-fourths of the several States within seven years from the date of its submission.

The 20th amendment to the Constitution was proposed by the Congress on March 2, 1932. It was declared, in a certificate by the Secretary of State, dated February 6, 1933, to have been ratified by the legislatures of 36 of the 48 States. The dates of ratification were: Virginia, March 4, 1932; New York, March 11, 1932; Mississippi, March 16, 1932; Arkansas, March 17, 1932; Kentucky, March 17, 1932; New Jersey, March 21, 1932; South Carolina, March 25, 1932; Michigan, March 31, 1932; Maine, April 1, 1932; Rhode Island, April 14, 1932; Illinois, April 21, 1932; Louisiana, June 22, 1932; West Virginia, July 30, 1932; Pennsylvania, August 11, 1932; Indiana, August 15, 1932; Texas, September 7, 1932; Alabama, September 13, 1932; California, January 4, 1933; North Carolina, January 5, 1933; North Dakota, January 9, 1933; Minnesota, January 12, 1933; Arizona, January 13, 1933; Montana, January 13, 1933; Nebraska, January 13, 1933; Oklahoma, January 13, 1933; Kansas, January 16, 1933; Oregon, January 16, 1933; Delaware, January 19, 1933; Washington, January 19, 1933; Wyoming, January 19, 1933; Iowa, January 20, 1933; South Dakota, January 20, 1933; Tennessee, January 20, 1933; Idaho, January 21, 1933; New Mexico, January 21, 1933; Georgia, January 23, 1933; Missouri, January 23, 1933; Ohio, January 23, 1933; Utah, January 23, 1933.

Ratification was completed on January 23, 1933.

The amendment was subsequently ratified by Massachusetts on January 24, 1933; Wisconsin, January 24, 1933; Colorado, January 24, 1933; Nevada, January 26, 1933; Connecticut, January 27, 1933; New Hampshire, January 31, 1933; Vermont, February 2, 1933; Maryland, March 24, 1933; Florida, April 26, 1933.

ARTICLE XXI.

SECTION 1. The eighteenth article of amendment to the Constitution of the United States is hereby repealed.

SECTION 2. The transportation or importation into any State, Territory, or possession of the United States for delivery or use therein of intoxicating liquors, in violation of the laws thereof, is hereby prohibited.

SECTION 3. This article shall be inoperative unless it shall have been ratified as an amendment to the Constitution by conventions in the several States, as provided in the Constitution, within seven years from the date of the submission hereof to the States by the Congress.

The 21st amendment to the Constitution was proposed by the Congress on February 20, 1933. It was declared, in a certificate of the Acting Secretary of State, dated December 5, 1933, to have been ratified by conventions in 36 of the 48 States. The dates of ratification were: Michigan, April 10, 1933; Wisconsin, April 25, 1933; Rhode Island, May 8, 1933; Wyoming, May 25, 1933; New Jersey, June 1, 1933; Delaware, June 24, 1933; Indiana, June 26, 1933; Massachusetts, June 26, 1933; New York, June 27, 1933; Illinois, July 10, 1933; Iowa, July 10, 1933; Connecticut, July 11, 1933; New Hampshire, July 11, 1933; California, July 24, 1933; West Virginia, July 25, 1933; Arkansas, August 1, 1933; Oregon, August 7, 1933; Alabama, August 8, 1933; Tennessee, August 11, 1933; Missouri, August 29, 1933; Arizona, September 5, 1933; Nevada, September 5, 1933; Vermont, September 23, 1933; Colorado, September 26, 1933; Washington, October 3, 1933; Minnesota, October 10, 1933; Idaho, October 17, 1933; Maryland, October 18, 1933; Virginia, October 25, 1933; New Mexico, November 2, 1933; Florida, November 14, 1933; Texas, November 24, 1933; Kentucky, November 27, 1933; Ohio, December 5, 1933; Pennsylvania, December 5, 1933; Utah, December 5, 1933.

Ratification was completed on December 5, 1933.

The amendment was subsequently ratified by Maine, on December 6, 1933, and by Montana, on August 6, 1934.

The amendment was rejected by South Carolina, on December 4, 1933.

ARTICLE XXII.

SECTION 1. No person shall be elected to the office of the President more than twice, and no person who has held the office of President, or acted as President, for more than two years of a term to which some other person was elected President shall be elected to the office of the President more than once. But this Article shall not apply to any person holding the office of President when this Article was proposed by the Congress, and shall not prevent any person who may be holding the office of President, or acting as President, during the term within which this Article becomes operative from holding the office of President or acting as President during the remainder of such term.

SECTION 2. This article shall be inoperative unless it shall have been ratified as an amendment to the Constitution by the legislatures of three-fourths of the several States within seven years from the date of its submission to the States by the Congress.

The 22d amendment to the Constitution was proposed by the Congress on March 21, 1947. It was declared, in a certificate by the Administrator of General Services, dated March 3, 1951, to have been ratified by the legislatures of 36 of the 48 States. The dates of ratification were: Maine, March 31, 1947; Michigan, March 31, 1947; Iowa, April 1, 1947; Kansas, April 1, 1947; New Hampshire, April 1, 1947; Delaware, April 2, 1947; Illinois, April 3, 1947; Oregon, April 3, 1947; Colorado, April 12, 1947; California, April 15, 1947; New Jersey, April 15, 1947; Vermont, April 15, 1947; Ohio, April 16, 1947; Wisconsin, April 16, 1947; Pennsylvania, April 29, 1947; Connecticut, May 21, 1947; Missouri, May 22, 1947; Nebraska, May 23, 1947; Virginia, January 28, 1948; Mississippi, February 12, 1948; New York, March 9, 1948; South Dakota, January 21, 1949; North Dakota, February 25, 1949; Louisiana, May 17, 1950; Montana, January 25, 1951; Indiana, January 29, 1951; Idaho, January 30, 1951; New Mexico, February 12, 1951; Wyoming, February 12, 1951; Arkansas, February 15, 1951; Georgia, February 17, 1951; Tennessee, February 20, 1951; Texas, February 22, 1951; Nevada, February 26, 1951; Utah, February 26, 1951; Minnesota, February 27, 1951.

Ratification was completed on February 27, 1951.

The amendment was subsequently ratified by North Carolina on February 28, 1951; South Carolina, March 13, 1951; Maryland, March 14, 1951; Florida, April 16, 1951; Alabama, May 4, 1951.

The amendment was rejected by Oklahoma in June 1947, and Massachusetts on June 9, 1949.

ARTICLE XXIII.

SECTION 1. The District constituting the seat of Government of the United States shall appoint in such manner as the Congress may direct:

A number of electors of President and Vice President equal to the whole number of Senators and Representatives in Congress to which the District would be entitled if it were a State, but in no event more than the least populous State; they shall be in addition to those appointed by the States, but they shall be considered, for the purposes of the election of President and Vice President, to be electors appointed by a State; and they shall meet in the District and perform such duties as provided by the twelfth article of amendment.

SECTION 2. The Congress shall have power to enforce this article by appropriate legislation.

The 23d amendment to the Constitution was proposed by the Congress on June 17, 1960. It was declared, in a certificate by the Administrator of General Services, to have been ratified by 38 of the 50 States. The dates of ratification were: Hawaii, June 23, 1960 (and that State made a technical correction to its resolution on June 30, 1960); Massachusetts, August 22, 1960; New Jersey,

December 19, 1960; New York, January 17, 1961; California, January 19, 1961; Oregon, January 27, 1961; Maryland, January 30, 1961; Idaho, January 31, 1961; Maine, January 31, 1961; Minnesota, January 31, 1961; New Mexico, February 1, 1961; Nevada, February 2, 1961; Montana, February 6, 1961; South Dakota, February 6, 1961; Colorado, February 8, 1961; Washington, February 9, 1961; West Virginia, February 9, 1961; Alaska, February 10, 1961; Wyoming, February 13, 1961; Delaware, February 20, 1961; Utah, February 21, 1961; Wisconsin, February 21, 1961; Pennsylvania, February 28, 1961; Indiana, March 3, 1961; North Dakota, March 3, 1961; Tennessee, March 6, 1961; Michigan, March 8, 1961; Connecticut, March 9, 1961; Arizona, March 10, 1961; Illinois, March 14, 1961; Nebraska, March 15, 1961; Vermont, March 15, 1961; Iowa, March 16, 1961; Missouri, March 20, 1961; Oklahoma, March 21, 1961; Rhode Island, March 22, 1961; Kansas, March 29, 1961; Ohio, March 29, 1961.

Ratification was completed on March 29, 1961.

The amendment was subsequently ratified by New Hampshire on March 30, 1961 (when that State annulled and then repeated its ratification of March 29, 1961).

The amendment was rejected by Arkansas on January 24, 1961.

ARTICLE XXIV

SECTION 1. The right of citizens of the United States to vote in any primary or other election for President or Vice President, for electors for President or Vice President, or for Senator or Representative in Congress, shall not be denied or abridged by the United States or any State by reason of failure to pay any poll tax or other tax.

SEC. 2. The Congress shall have power to enforce this article by appropriate legislation.

The 24th amendment to the Constitution was proposed by the Congress on August 27, 1962. It was declared, in a certificate of the Administrator of General Services, dated February 4, 1964, to have been ratified by the legislatures of 38 of the 50 States. The dates of ratification were: Illinois, November 14, 1962; New Jersey, December 3, 1962; Oregon, January 25, 1963; Montana, January 28, 1963; West Virginia, February 1, 1963; New York, February 4, 1963; Maryland, February 6, 1963; California, February 7, 1963; Alaska, February 11, 1963; Rhode Island, February 14, 1963; Indiana, February 19, 1963; Utah, February 20, 1963; Michigan, February 20, 1963; Colorado, February 21, 1963; Ohio, February 27, 1963; Minnesota, February 27, 1963; New Mexico, March 5, 1963; Hawaii, March 6, 1963; North Dakota, March 7, 1963; Idaho, March 8, 1963; Washington, March 14, 1963; Vermont, March 15, 1963; Nevada, March 19, 1963; Connecticut, March 20, 1963; Tennessee, March 21, 1963; Pennsylvania, March 25, 1963; Wisconsin, March 26, 1963; Kansas, March 28, 1963; Massachusetts, March 28, 1963; Nebraska, April 4, 1963; Florida, April 18, 1963; Iowa, April 24, 1963; Delaware, May 1, 1963; Missouri, May 13, 1963; New Hampshire, June 12, 1963; Kentucky, June 27, 1963; Maine, January 16, 1964; South Dakota, January 23, 1964.

Ratification was completed on January 23, 1964.

The amendment was rejected by Mississippi on December 20, 1962.

Notes

2. Civil Rights in the Supreme Court

1. 1 Cranch 137, 2 L. Ed. 60 (1803).
2. *West Virginia* v. *Barnette*, 319 U.S. 624 (1943).
3. *Slaughter House Cases*, 16 Wall. 36, 21 L. Ed. 394 (1873).
4. 268 U.S. 652 (1925).
5. 302 U.S. 319 (1937).
6. *Ashwander* v. *Tennessee Valley Authority*, 297 U.S. 288, 346 (1936).
7. *Terminiello* v. *Chicago*, 337 U.S. 1 (1949).
8. *Osborn* v. *The Bank of the United States*, 9 Wheat. 739 (1824).
9. *United States* v. *Butler*, 297 U.S. 1, 87 (1935).

3. Freedom of Religious Conviction

1. See discussion in *Engel* v. *Vitale*, 370 U.S. 421 (1962).
2. *Cantwell* v. *Connecticut*, 310 U.S. 296 (1940).
3. *Everson* v. *Board of Education*, 330 U.S. 1, 15 (1947).
4. *Lorcaso* v. *Watkins*, 367 U.S. 488 (1961).
5. 330 U.S. 1, 15 (1947).
6. *Illinois* ex rel. *McCollum* v. *Board of Education*, 333 U.S. 203 (1948).
7. *Zorach* v. *Clauson*, 343 U.S. 306 (1952).
8. *Engel* v. *Vitale*, 370 U.S. 421 (1962).
9. *Abington Township School District* v. *Schempp*, 374 U.S. 203 (1963).
10. *De Spain* et al. v. *DeKalb County Community School District*, 428, et. al., decided by Circuit Court of Appeals, Seventh Circuit, July 26, 1967, certiorari denied, January 22, 1968.
11. Article XI, Section 3.
12. 374 U.S. 203 (1963).
13. *Flast* et al. v. *Cohen*, No. 416, 36 *U.S. Law Week* 4601 (1968).
14. *Board of Education* v. *Allen*, No. 660, 36 *U.S. Law Week* 4538 (1968).
15. Conference of National Community Relations Advisory Council, San Francisco, (July 1, 1968).
16. *Ibid.*
17. *McGowan* v. *Maryland*, 366 U.S. 420 (1961).
18. *Reynolds* v. *United States*, 98 U.S. 145 (1879).
19. *West Virginia State Board of Education* v. *Barnette*, 319 U.S. 624 (1943).
20. *Taylor* v. *Mississippi*, 319 U.S. 583 (1943).
21. *Minersville School District* v. *Gobitis*, 310 U.S. 586 (1940).
22. *Cantwell* v. *Connecticut*, 310 U.S. 326 (1940).
23. *Cox* v. *New Hampshire*, 312 U.S. 569 (1941).
24. *Chaplinsky* v. *New Hampshire*, 315 U.S. 568 (1942).
25. *Poulos* v. *New Hampshire*, 345 U.S. 395 (1953).
26. *Schenk* v. *United States*, 249 U.S. 47 (1919).
27. 73 F. 2d 357 (Circuit Court of Appeals, Ga.), 194 F. 2d 1011, certiorari denied 343 U.S. 980, rehearing denied 344 U.S. 849.

28. 325 U.S. 561 (1945).
29. 283 U.S. 605 (1931).
30. 348 U.S. 385 (1955).
31. Discussed in Dorsen and Rodovsky, "On Selective Conscientious Objection," *Columbia University Forum*, Spring, 1968, pp. 44-45.
32. See *New York Times*, July 30, 1968, p. 78.
33. *Clay* v. *United States*, certiorari granted July 5, 1968, 36 *U.S. Law Week* 2693.
34. See *New York Times*, April 18, 1968, p. 10.
35. 249 U.S. 47 (1919).

4. Freedom of Expression

1. Oliver Wendell Holmes, dissenting in *Abrams* v. *United States*, 250 U.S. 616, at 630 (1919).
2. *Gitlow* v. *New York*, 268 U.S. 652 (1925) ; *Near* v. *Minnesota*, 283 U.S. 697 (1931).
3. *Burstyn* v. *Wilson*, 343 U.S. 495 (1952).
4. *Schenk* v. *United States*, 249 U.S. 47, 52 (1919).
5. *Abrams* v. *United States*, 250 U.S. 616 (1919).
6. *Frohwerk* v. *United States*, 249 U.S. 204 (1919).
7. *Debs* v. *United States*, 249 U.S. 211 (1919).
8. Compare *Abrams* v. *United States*, 250 U.S. 616 (1919) to *Schaefer* v. *United States*, 251 U.S. 466 (1920).
9. *Herndon* v. *Lowry*, 301 U.S. 242 (1937).
10. 268 U.S. 652 (1925).
11. *United States* v. *Caroline Products Co.*, 304 U.S. 144 (1938).
12. *Palco* v. *Connecticut*, 302 U.S. 319 (1937).
13. *Thomas* v. *Collins*, 323 U.S. 516 (1945).
14. 337 U.S. 1 (1949).
15. 340 U.S. 315 (1951).
16. 341 U.S. 494 (1951).
17. *Ibid.*, p. 510.
18. *Yates* v. *United States*, 354 U.S. 298 (1957).
19. 354 U.S. 476, 489 (1957).
20. 354 U.S. 746, 490 (1957).
21. 274 U.S. 380 (1927).
22. 354 U.S. 298 (1957).
23. *Roth* v. *United States*, 354 U.S. 476 (1957).
24. *Alberts* v. *California*, 354 U.S. 746 (1957).
25. *Butler* v. *Michigan*, 352 U.S. 380 (1957).
26. *Manual Enterprises* v. *Day*, 370 U.S. 478 (1962).
27. S. Ct. 1414 (1966).
28. *Ginsberg* v. *New York*, Nos. 14 & 17, 36 *U.S. Law Week* 4295, decided April 22, 1968.
29. Gaylin, "The Prickly Problems of Pornography," 77 *Yale Law Journal* 452 (1968).
30. *Ginzburg* v. *United States*, 383 U.S. 463 (1966).
31. *Near* v. *Minnesota*, 283 U.S. 697 (1931).
32. *Times Film Corp.* v. *Chicago*, 365 U.S. 43 (1961).
33. *Friedman* v. *Maryland*, 380 U.S. 436 (1957).
34. *Interstate Circuit, Inc.* v. *Dallas*, Nos. 56 & 64, 36 *U.S. Law Week* 4309, decided April 22, 1968.
35. *Kingsley Books* v. *Brown*, 354 U.S. 436 (1957).
36. *Bantam Books* v. *Sullivan*, 372 U.S. 58 (1963).

37. See "Fair Trial—Free Press," a series in the *New York Law Journal*, beginning March 19, 1968.
38. Discussed in Leavitt, "Studied Ignorance—The Mainspring of a Fair Trial: The Press and Pretrial Prejudice," *New York Law Journal*, May 29 and 30, 1968.
39. *New York Times* v. *Sullivan*, 376 U.S. 254 (1964).
40. *Phil A. St. Amant* v. *Herman A. Thompson*, No. 517, 36 *U.S. Law Week* 333, decided April 29, 1968.
41. *Pickering* v. *School Board*, No. 510, 36 *U.S. Law Week* 4495, decided June 3, 1968.
42. *Curtis Publishing Company* v. *Butts*, 388 U.S. 130 (1967).
43. *New York Times*, May 12, 1968, p. 6-E.

5. Rights of Assembly and Petition

1. *DeJonge* v. *Oregon*, 299 U.S. 353 (1937); *Douglas* v. *City of Jenett*, 319 U.S. 157 (1943).
2. *Brotherhood of Railroad Trainmen* v. *Virginia* ex rel. *Virginia State Bar Association*, 377 U.S. 1 (1961); *National Association for the Advancement of Colored People* v. *Button*, 371 U.S. 415 (1963).
3. *Bates* v. *Little Rock*, 361 U.S. 516 (1960).
4. 299 U.S. 353 (1937).
5. *United Public Workers* v. *Mitchell*, 330 U.S. 75, 79 (1947).
6. 307 U.S. 496 (1939).
7. 314 U.S. 247 (1941).
8. *Thomas* v. *Collins*, 323 U.S. 516 (1945).
9. 310 U.S. 98 (1940).
10. *International Brotherhood of Teamsters* v. *Vogt, Inc.*, 354 U.S. 284 (1957).
11. *Milk Wagon Drivers Union* v. *Meadowmoor Dairies*, 312 U.S. 287 (1941).
12. *American Federation of Labor* v. *Swing*, 312 U.S. 321 (1941).
13. *United States* v. *Rumely*, 345 U.S. 41 (1953).
14. *United States* v. *Harris* et al., 347 U.S. 612 (1954).
15. *Becker* v. *Deneco Corp.*, No. 145, 36 *U.S. Law Week* 3229, decided Dec. 4, 1967.
16. *United States* v. *Robel*, No. 8, 36 *U.S. Law Week* 4060, decided Dec. 11, 1967.
17. *Schneider* v. *Smith*, No. 196, 36 *U.S. Law Week* 4131, decided Jan. 16, 1968.
18. *Gardner* v. *Broderick*, No. 635, 36 *U.S. Law Week* 4536, decided June 10, 1968.
19. 355 U.S. 115 (1957).
20. 354 U.S. 178 (1957).
21. *Aptheker* v. *Secretary of State*, 378 U.S. 500 (1964).
22. 379 U.S. 536 (1965).
23. See "Right to Demonstrate," *Columbia Journal of Law and Social Problems*, October 24, 1966.
24. *Cox* v. *New Hampshire*, 312 U.S. 569 (1941); *Cox* v. *Louisiana*, 379 U.S. 536 (1965); *International Brotherhood of Teamsters* v. *Vogt, Inc.*, 354 U.S. 284 (1957); *Kovacs* v. *Cooper*, 336 U.S. 77 (1949).
25. *Feiner* v. *New York*, 340 U.S. 315 (1951).
26. 372 U.S. 229 (1963).
27. 279 U.S. 536 (1965).
28. *New York Times*, January 21, 1968, p. 1.
29. *United States* v. *O'Brien*, No. 232, 36 *U.S. Law Week*, 4469, decided May 27, 1968.

6. Security of Person and Home

1. *Presser* v. *Illinois*, 116 U.S. 542 (1886).
2. *United States* v. *Cruikshank*, 92 U.S. 542 (1876).
3. *United States* v. *Miller*, 307 U.S. 174 (1939) ; *Todd* v. *United States*, 319 U.S. 463 (1943).
4. *United States* v. *Valenzuela*, 95 F. Supp. 363, 367 (S. D. Cal., 1951).
5. Argument concerning writs of assistance, Boston Court, Feb. 24, 1761.
6. *Boyd* v. *United States*, 116 U.S. 616 (1886).
7. *Wolf* v. *Colorado*, 338 U.S. 25 (1949).
8. *Kelley* v. *United States*, 298 F. 2d 310 (Court of Appeals, District Court, 1961).
9. *Draper* v. *United States*, 358 U.S. 307 (1959).
10. *Wong Sun* v. *United States*, 371 U.S. 471 (1963).
11. *Wheeler* v. *Nesbitt*, 65 U.S. 544, 552 (1860).
12. *Peyton* v. *Rowe*, No. 802, 36 *U.S. Law Week* 4462, decided May 20, 1968.
13. *Carafas* v. *La Valee*, No. 71, 36 *U.S. Law Week* 4409, decided May 20, 1968.
14. *New York Times*, July 20, 1967, p. 1; see also "Riot Control and the Fourth Amendment," *Harvard Law Review*, January, 1968.
15. *Johnson* v. *United States*, 333 U.S. 1013 (1948).
16. *Shapiro* v. *United States*, 335 U.S. 1 (1948).
17. *Carroll* v. *United States*, 267 U.S. 132 (1925).
18. *Weeks* v. *United States*, 232 U.S. 383 (1914) ; *United States* v. *Rabinowitz*, 339 U.S. 56 (1950) ; *Go-Bart Importing Co.* v. *United States*, 282 U.S. 344 (1931).
19. *United States* v. *Rabinowitz*, 339 U.S. 56 (1950).
20. *Hayden* v. *Warden*, 385 U.S. 926 (1966).
21. *Katz* v. *United States*, No. 35, 36 *U.S. Law Week* 4080, decided Dec. 18, 1967.
22. *New York Times*, June 18, 1968, p. 33.
23. *Terry* v. *Ohio*, No. 67, 36 *U.S. Law Week* 4578, decided June 10, 1968.
24. *Ibid.*
25. *Sibron* v. *New York*, No. 63, and *Peter* v. *New York*, No. 74, 36 *U.S. Law Week* 4589, decided June 10, 1968.
26. *Boyd* v. *United States*, 116 U.S. 616 (1886).
27. 232 U.S. 383, 393 (1914).
28. 308 U.S. 338 (1939).
29. 364 U.S. 206 (1960).
30. *Rochin* v. *California*, 342 U.S. 165 (1952).
31. 367 U.S. 643 (1961).
32. *Bumper* v. *North Carolina*, No. 1016, 36 *U.S. Law Week* 4513, decided June 3, 1968.

7. The Right to Life, Liberty and Property

1. See C. H. McIlwain, "Due Process of Law in the Magna Carta," 14 *Columbia Law Review* 27 (1914).
2. W. W. Willoughby, *Constitution of the United States* 1686 (2d ed., 1929).
3. 110 U.S. 516 (1884).
4. *United States* v. *Moreland*, 258 U.S. 433 (1922) ; *Mackin* v. *United States*, 117 U.S. 348 (1886).
5. *Norris* v. *Alabama*, 294 U.S. 587 (1935).
6. *Ruthenberg* v. *United States*, Sec. 1, 245 U.S. 480 (1918).
7. *United States* v. *Hess*, 1924 U.S. 483 (1888) ; *United States* v. *Simmons*, 96 U.S. 360 (1878).

8. *Stewart* v. *United States,* 366 U.S. 1 (1966).
9. *Reade* v. *United States,* 355 U.S. 184 (1957).
10. *Downum* v. *United States,* 372 U.S. 734 (1963).
11. 302 U.S. 319 (1937).
12. *Brock* v. *North Carolina,* 344 U.S. 423 (1953).
13. *Brown* v. *Mississippi,* 397 U.S. 278 (1936).
14. *Malloy* v. *Hogan,* 378 U.S. 1 (1964).
15. *Brown* v. *Mississippi,* 297 U.S. 278, 285 (1936).
16. 347 U.S. 556 (1954).
17. 360 U.S. 315 (1959).
18. *Haines* v. *Washington,* 373 U.S. 503 (1963).
19. 384 U.S. 436.
20. *Twining* v. *New Jersey,* 211 U.S. 78 (1908) ; *Adamson* v. *California,* 332 U.S. 46 (1947).
21. *Malloy* v. *Hogan,* 378 U.S. 1 (1964).
22. *Griffin* v. *California,* 380 U.S. 609 (1965).
23. *Quinn* v. *United States,* 349 U.S. 155 (1955).
24. *Blau* v. *United States,* 340 U.S. 149 (1950).
25. *Brown* v. *Walker,* 161 U.S. 591 (1896) ; *Ullmann* v. *United States,* 350 U.S. 522 (1956).
26. *Murphy* v. *Waterfront Commission,* 378 U.S. 52, 77-78 (1964).
27. *Gardiner* v. *Broderick,* No. 635, 36 *U.S. Law Week* 536, decided June 10, 1968.
28. *Uniformed Sanitation Men's Association, Inc.* v. *Commissioner,* No. 823, 36 *U.S. Law Week* 4534, decided June 10, 1968.
29. *George Campbell Painting Corp.* v. *Reid* et al., No. 673, 36 *U.S. Law Week* 4533, decided June 10, 1968.
30. *Rochin* v. *California,* 342 U.S. 165, 169 (1942).
31. *Galvan* v. *Press,* 347 U.S. 522, 530 (1954).
32. Daniel Webster, *Constitutional Limitations,* 736 (8th ed., 1927).
33. *Kent* et al. v. *Dulles,* 357 U.S. 116 (1958).
34. *Aptheker* v. *Secretary of State,* 378 U.S. 500 (1964).
35. *Zemel* v. *Rusk,* 381 U.S. 1 (1965).
36. *Griswold* v. *Connecticut,* 381 U.S. 479 (1965).
37. *Baron* v. *Baltimore,* 32 U.S. 243 (1833).
38. *Chicago, Burlington & Quincy Railroad Co.* v. *Chicago,* 166 U.S. 776, 258 (1897).
39. *United States,* ex rel. *Tennessee Valley Authority* v. *Welch,* 327 U.S. 546, 551-552 (1946).
40. *Berman* v. *Parker,* 348 U.S. 26 (1954).
41. *United States* v. *Cansby,* 328 U.S. 56 (1946).
42. *Chicago, Burlington & Quincy Railroad Co.* v. *Chicago,* 166 U.S. 776, 258 (1897).
43. *Armstrong* v. *United States,* 364 U.S. 40, 49 (1960).

8. Fair Trials in Criminal and Civil Cases

1. *Duncan* v. *Louisiana,* No. 410, 36 *U.S. Law Week* 4414, decided May 20, 1958.
2. *New York Times,* June 1, 1968, p. 15.
3. *Singer* v. *United States,* 380 U.S. 24 (1965) ; *Adams* v. *United States* ex rel. *McCann,* 317 U.S. 269 (1942).
4. *Singer* v. *United States,* 380 U.S. 24 (1965).
5. *In re Provo,* 17 F.R.D. 183 (D. Md., 1965), aff'd., 350 U.S. 857 (1955).
6. *In re Oliver,* 333 U.S. 257 (1948).
7. *Estes* v. *Texas,* 85 S. Ct. 1628 (1965).

8. *Patton* v. *Mississippi*, 332 U.S. 463 (1947); *Smith* v. *Texas*, 311 U.S. 128 (1940); *Strander* v. *West Virginia*, 100 U.S. 303 (1880); compare *Hoyt* v. *Florida*, 368 U.S. 57 (1961).
9. *Witherspoon* v. *Illinois*, No. 1015, 36 *U.S. Law Week* 4504, decided June 3, 1968.
10. *Hyde* v. *United States*, 225 U.S. 347 (1912).
11. *Johnson* v. *United States*, 351 U.S. 215 (1956).
12. *Travis* v. *United States*, 364 U.S. 631 (1961).
13. *Pointer* v. *Texas*, 380 U.S. 400 (1965).
14. *Douglas* v. *Alabama*, 380 U.S. 415 (1965).
15. *Feuguer* v. *United States*, 302 F. 2d 214 (Court of Appeals 8, 1962), certiorari denied, 371 U.S. 872 (1962).
16. 372 U.S. 335 (1963).
17. *Massiah* v. *United States*, 377 U.S. 201 (1964).
18. 378 U.S. 478 (1964).
19. *Miranda* v. *Arizona*, 384 U.S. 436 (1966).
20. *Minneapolis & St. Louis Railroad* v. *Bombolis*, 242 U.S. 211 (1916).
21. *National Labor Relations Board* v. *United States*, 231 U.S. 9 (1913).
22. *Capitol Traction Co.* v. *Hoff*, 174 U.S. 1 (1899).
23. *Galloway* v. *United States*, 319 U.S. 372 (1943).
24. *Lavender* v. *Kurn*, 327 U.S. 645 (1946).
25. *New York Times* v. *Sullivan*, 376 U.S. 254 (1964).
26. *Pilkington* v. *Circuit Court of Howell County, Missouri*, 324 F. 2d 45, 46 (Court of Appeals 8, 1963).
27. *Robinson* v. *California*, 370 U.S. 660 (1962).
28. *United States* ex rel. *Bryant* v. *Fay*, 211 F. Supp. 812 (S.D.N.Y., 1962), certiorari denied, 375 U.S. 852 (1963); *Redding* v. *Pate*, 220 F. Supp. 124 (N.D. Ill., 1963).
29. *United States* ex rel. *Watkins* v. *Vissering*, 184 F. Supp. 529 (E.D. Va., 1960).
30. 342 U.S. 1 (1951).
31. Ex parte *Watkins*, 32 U.S. 568 (1833).
32. *Canon* v. *Delaware*, 196 A. 2d 399 (Del., 1963).
33. *Weems* v. *United States*, 217 U.S. 349 (1910).
34. *Robinson* v. *California*, 370 U.S. 660, 666 (1962).
35. *New York Times*, June 18, 1968, pp. 1, 33.
36. 356 U.S. 86 (1958).
37. *Wilberson* v. *Utah*, 99 U.S. 130 (1879).
38. *Hernandez* v. *State*, 32 P. 2d 18 (Arizona, 1934).
39. *Louisiana* ex rel. *Francis* v. *Resweb*, 329 U.S. 459 (1947).
40. *Chessman* v. *Teets*, 354 U.S. 156 (1957).
41. *Witherspoon* v. *Illinois*, No. 1015, 36 *U.S. Law Week* 4504, decided June 3, 1968.
42. Michigan (1847); Rhode Island (1852); Wisconsin (1853); Maine (1876); Minnesota (1911); North Dakota (1915); Alaska and Hawaii (1957); Oregon (1964); West Virginia, Vermont, Iowa, and New York (1965).

9. Civil Rights After the Civil War

1. *Slaughter House Cases*, 16 Wall. 36, 21 L. Ed. 394 (1873).
2. 1883.
3. *Plessy* v. *Ferguson*, 163 U.S. 537 (1896).
4. *Palco* v. *Connecticut*, 302 U.S. 319 (1937).
5. *Adamson* v. *California*, 372 U.S. 46 (1947).
6. *Smith* v. *Allwright*, 321 U.S. 649 (1949).

7. *Harman* v. *Forssenius,* 235 Fed. Supp. 66 (1964).
8. 369 U.S. 186 (1962).
9. 372 U.S. 368 (1963).
10. No. 39, 36 *U.S. Law Week* 4257, decided April 1, 1968.
11. *Shelley* v. *Kraemer,* 334 U.S. 1 (1948); *Hurd* v. *Hodge,* 334 U.S. 24 (1948);
    Banons v. *Jackson,* 346 U.S. 249 (1953).
12. *Civil Rights Cases,* 109 U.S. 3 (1883); *Buchanan* v. *Warley,* 245 U.S. 60
    (1917); *Corrigan* v. *Buckley,* 271 U.S. 323 (1926).
13. *Shelley* v. *Kraemer,* 334 U.S. 1 (1948).
14. *Daisy* v. *Stuyvesant,* 299 N.Y. 512 (1949); 339 U.S. 981 (1950).
15. *Black* v. *Cutters Laboratories,* 351 U.S. 292 (1956); see also *Rice* v. *Sioux
    City Park,* 349 U.S. 70 (1955).
16. *Jones* v. *Alfred H. Mayer, Co.,* No. 645, 36 *U.S. Law Week* 4661, decided
    June 17, 1968.
17. 163 U.S. 537 (1896).
18. Robert J. Harris, *The Quest for Equality* (Louisiana State University Press,
    1960), Chap. 4.
19. 313 U.S. 80 (1941).
20. 328 U.S. 373 (1946).
21. *Bob-Lo Excursion Co.* v. *Michigan,* 333 U.S. 28 (1948); *Henderson* v. *United
    States,* 339 U.S. 816 (1950).
22. *Missouri* ex rel. *Gaines* v. *Canada,* 305 U.S. 337 (1938).
23. 339 U.S. 629 (1950).
24. *McLaurin* v. *Oklahoma State Regents,* 339 U.S. 637 (1950).
25. 347 U.S. 483 (1954).
26. *Brown* v. *Board of Education,* 349 U.S. 294 (1955).
27. *Avery* v. *Midland County,* No. 39, 36 *U.S. Law Week* 4257, decided April 1,
    1968.
28. 109 U.S. 3 (1883).
29. *Burton* v. *Wilmington Parking Authority,* 365 U.S. 715 (1961).
30. *Peterson* v. *City of Greenville,* 373 U.S. 244 (1963); *Lombard* v. *State of
    Louisiana,* 373 U.S. 276 (1963).
31. 378 U.S. 130 (1964).
32. 378 U.S. 153 (1964).
33. *Heart of Atlanta Motel* v. *United States,* 379 U.S. 241 (1964).
34. *Ibid.*

10. Civil Rights and the Constitution in the Sixth Decade

1. See Chap. 9, p. 59.
2. See, e.g., *Civil Rights Cases,* 109 U.S. 3 (1883).
3. See, e.g., *Brown* v. *Board of Education,* 347 U.S. 483 (1954).
4. *Bell* v. *Maryland,* 378 U.S. 226 (1964).
5. James Madison Lecture at New York University Law School (March 29, 1967).
   Reprinted in *New York Law Journal,* April 5, 1967, p. 4.
6. Adolf A. Berle, *The Three Faces of Power* (New York, Harcourt, Brace &
   World, 1967), pp. vii-viii.
7. 374 U.S. 483 (1954).
8. 378 U.S. 226 (1964).
9. 369 U.S. 186 (1962).
10. *Avery* v. *Midland County,* No. 39, 36 *U.S. Law Week* 4257, decided April 1,
    1968.
11. 334 U.S. 1 (1948).

12. *Steele* v. *Louisville and Nashville Railroad Co.*, 323 U.S. 192 (1944).
13. 46 *Yale Law Journal* 523 (1946).
14. Berle, *op. cit.*, p. viii.
15. Carpenter Lectures at Columbia University (March 21, 1968).
16. *Brown* v. *Board of Education*, 347 U.S. 483 (1954).
17. See H. H. Remmers and D. H. Radler, *The American Teenager* (Indianapolis, Bobbs-Merrill Co., Inc., 1957), Chap. 8, pp. 16-17.

Index

213